Overcoming

INHERITED
FAMILY TRAUMA
WORKBOOK

Dr Corin Wellington

Dr Corin Wellington

Overcoming

INHERITED
FAMILY TRAUMA
WORKBOOK

e

OVERCOMING INHERITED FAMILY TRAUMA WORKBOOK

Light house publishers are based in the United States.
Light house publishers published in Australia.
Light house publishers published in the United Kingdom.
Cover design by: Precious Matilda
Interior design by: nwosu paul Chibuike
Indexer: light house publishers

The author of this book does not dispense medical advice or prescribe the use of any technique as treatment for physical, emotional, or medical problems without the advice of a physician, either directly or indirectly. The intent of the author is only to offer general information to help you in your quest for emotional, physical, and spiritual well-being. In the event you use any of the information in this workbook for yourself, the author and the publisher assume no responsibility for your actions.

.

I dedicate this book to my
Mum - Mrs Mabel Mma
I love you mum

Table of content

INTRODUCTION

How To Use This Workbook

Inherited trauma is a topic which has little recognition, yet its effect is visible in the life of many. Victims of inherited trauma usually suffer from symptoms ranging from anxiety, fear, financial worries, depression, illness and even unhappy relationships, but the solution is farfetched from the average therapeutic sessions and mental health books.

Do you suffer from unexplained fear, worry, anxiety and various other emotional instability, or in most cases, you see yourself ensnared in a continuous pattern of reasoning that has disturbed your general wellbeing and level of success? Worry no more. The answer is in inherited family trauma. And through this workbook, your healing is certain.

How to read the book and work with the workbook

This book comprises two broad categories. The first is an introduction to trauma, its origin, symptoms, and how it affects you. While the second category primarily focuses on overcoming these traumas, using some proven therapeutic techniques and exercises.

PREFIX;

Please note; Some information in this book may at some point seem absurd or irrelevant, irrespective of the case, it is helpful that you give them a trial as they have been proven by many therapist and mental health diagnostics institutes to be effective and appropriate. Without doubt, every information written has, at some point, helped different individuals to recover from the effects of their inherited emotions.

Ensure to do every exercise listed with exception if they contradict your religious belief and practices.

To get the best out of this book, it is appropriate to approach with a rational mind and a desire to gain insight on the subject and how effective its tool would be to your mental health.

The workbook part of this book is based on communication and talk therapy. We simplified the content to be like a real therapeutic session. You will be expected to write, draw, recite, declare and even implore your imaginations. It's best advisable to dedicate a notebook to document and continue the exercises, especially where the space provided is insufficient. At some point, you are required to photocopy a page or two and continue the exercises repeatedly. It is important that you do all these, as they are important for your recovery.

What you will learn from these workbooks

- An understanding of family history coupled with exercises to help you unveil yours.
- How to create deep connections with your family
- Overcome the inherited emotions that may affect your present reactions and behaviours
- Effective ways and practices to overcome inherited trauma

- Proven techniques to taking control of your emotions and standing up to your fears
- Several therapeutic methods and exercise to remain free from inherited trauma

See you on the other side of freedom

PREFIX;

About the author

Dr Corin wellington is the director and founder of Epigenetic transformation institute Utah. a trained inherited family therapist (IFT), a sought-after lecturer, a certified mediator and regression therapist. He is also a father of two. His works have been featured on popular media house like sounds true, The Huffington Post and Goop.

Dr Corin wellington specializes in trauma-related symptoms like anxieties, obsessive thoughts, fears, panic disorders, bipolar and other chronic related conditions.

Born into a family with a history of being survivors of the holocaust, DR Corin wellington suffered from various inherited emotions ranging from fear, panics, and chronic anxieties. During one of his interviews on Live tv when he was asked how it all started and what triggered his interest on the subject? He said... while growing up, my dad would always tell us stories his dad told him, how his grandfather was victimized in the camp of the Nazis. These stories were extremely hurtful and usually made him cry. Though the grandfather died a few years after he was rescued, the memories had caused various levels of depression to his father, who died early as well.

Caught in a web premature death and the depression that accompanied the memories, he had to seek help. During this process, he was introduced to the subject from which he developed interest and pursued it to mastery. He did his PhD and got certified to operate as a therapist.

As a witness on the severity of inherited trauma, he had helped trained many therapists and various individuals in dealing with inherited emotions accompanied with a trauma from family history

PREFIX

THE FIRST STEP TO HEALING.

Welcome to therapy!

Most people see therapy as a recommendation for people with severe cases of dysfunctionality. hearing the word therapy sends shivers of severity down their spines. Other people see therapy as an agenda for weak people who can't handle their own shits. Little do they know that the word therapy goes beyond having an official meeting with trained personnel. But exist in various forms, including spirituality, religion, prayer, music therapy, play therapy and even talk therapy. All these forms of therapy are done day by day without you knowing.

What then is therapy, according to oxford dictionary, therapy is the treatment of mental disorders using psychological means. It is a treatment intended to relieve or heal a disorder. In simpler terms, therapy is a safe place to help you feel better about upsetting or confusing events that you might have experienced.

In therapy, you will get to draw, write, talk, and play out your experiences as you are being guided into overcoming it. In this book we will implore a unique form of therapy called bibliotherapy, where we would ask you questions, put you through guided exercises, affirmations and other therapeutic tools effective in overcoming inherited emotions.

You are welcome to therapy. Please get your pen, marker and notebook.

Your therapy starts now.

About you

In this section, we will examine your core problems, starting with saying a thing or two about your immediate family, your reason for recovery, including your pains and worries. In this session, you are guided to identify and highlight areas where you need help the most. Express yourself in the best possible way. Note that the more open you are, the greater chances of your recovery.

Go ahead, describe a thing or two about you and your family and how you or they are being affected by inherited trauma.

You can as well pause these exercises and skip to CHAPTER ONE, where you will be taught all about inherited trauma and why the disorder is visible in the life of many.

About your family

The focus of these books is on inherited family trauma. And it's necessary that you describe your immediate family. What are some things you like about your family? What do you and your family like to do together? Are there any negative or painful memories write them down in the space provided?

_____

_____

_____

_____

_____

Have you experienced any personal traumatic event?

Most time, in looking for clues from family histories, we can start by re-examining ourselves. Have you experienced any personal traumatic event before? If yes, describe them. You can as well come back to this exercise, maybe after gaining an understanding on the subject. Describe your experience in this space below.

_____

_____

_____

_____

_____

_____

_____

_____

_____

What do you want out of trauma recovery?

Abuse, they say, is inevitable when purpose of a thing is not known. What do you want to gain from reading this book? What are your expectations? What pain do you want freedom from? Be free and express yourself in the section that follows.
List 3-5 things you would want to achieve from this book

PREFIX;

1. _____
2. _____
3. _____
4. _____
5. _____
6. _____

For each information on the list, explain why you want it:

1. _____
2. _____
3. _____
4. _____
5. _____
6. _____

Tell us how your life would be different if you actualised it.

1. _____
2. _____
3. _____

4.

5.

6.

What would have to be changed for you to do that thing?

1.

2.

3.

4.

5.

6.

The first thing you would have to do is describe the item on the list.

1.

2.

3.

4.

5.

To help you achieve the goal, describe what resources you would need, including people.

PREFIX;

1. _____

2. _____

3. _____

4. _____

5. _____

What qualities do you want in yourself?

List 3-5 qualities you want to have when you have completed your trauma recovery process: e.g. *I want to be more outspoken; I want to be bold, etc.*

1. _____

2. _____

3. _____

4. _____

5. _____

For each information on the list, explain why you want it:

1. _____

2. _____

3. _____

4.

5.

For each item on the list, explain what would have to change for you to gain that thing:

1.

2.

3.

4.

5.

If you had those qualities today, how would they help you in your recovery process?

1.

2.

3.

4.

Watch your belief, they might limit you

Your belief about therapy and inherited trauma can limit your progress as you embark on your journey to overcoming them.

PREFIX;

What do you believe? Do you believe inherited family trauma is real, or you see it as a vague subject? Are you fully convinced you can overcome the distractions and commit to applying the strategies required— using the various therapeutic tools? If not, you have a role to play in developing your belief to match your expectations. Recovering from inherited trauma is difficult when your beliefs are not aligned on the path of recovery.

how strongly do you agree with the following statements? Rate your belief on a scale of 1—10:

1. I believe inherited family trauma can be overcome.
   Rating _____

2. My unexplained emotions may have a connection to my family's history.
   3. Rating _____

4. I believe inherited family trauma is real and inevitable.
   Rating _____

5. I believe I have what it takes to overcome these traumas and take control of my life and emotions.
   Rating _____

 If you rate anything less than a 10 on any of those questions, ask yourself: What would it take to move that belief up ONE notch?

When you identify what that thing is, go get it! The believe statements above are examples of what you should be thinking. Now.

What other believe is rattling around in your mind? For trauma recovery, either positive or negative, write them down below: if none please skip to the next page.

_____

_____

_____

_____

_____

_____

From the above list, identify the various negative questions that may interfere with your recovery process and reward it with something more positive.

A negative question like "I don't think trauma can be overcome," should be switched with a more positive thought like "I will have to work very hard to overcome my trauma."

Now it's your turn list out positive beliefs and expectations that you should swap with your negative thoughts and criticising inner voice.

_____

_____

_____

_____

_____

_____

_____

PREFIX;

Section one:

CONNECTING THE DOTS

CHAPTER ONE

Inherited Family Trauma Web

Traumas are often frightening, life-threatening, or violent events that can happen to any individual, family, or group of people. The word "trauma" is coined from the Greek word **τραύμα,** which means "wound." It is an experience in one's life that causes serious harm, maybe physical, mental, or emotional. It's usually disturbing and can make an individual lose control of the present situation. Traumas often appear in two primary forms, the first being very severe and the other less severe. The severe ones may appear in many forms, such as the death of a parent, sexual abuse of a growing teen, bullying and physical abuse, etc. Therapists describe this type of trauma as **the "Big T" trauma.** The less severe incidents include the breaking of an arm, loss of property through armed robbery, or any other incident which may cause severe emotional damage to the victims but whose effects are not usually life-threatening. This is referred to as **"little T" trauma.**

Trauma is an emotional response to a hurtful event, in its simplest form. It can be rape, natural disaster, loss of life, etc. Its effects may persist for a long time, leaving an indelible mark on the body of its victim. Traumas experienced by parents leave a chemical imprint on the genetic composition of the person experiencing them and get passed down from there (Embrey: 2013). children of parents who survived traumatic events such as natural disaster, physical abuse, and rape are likely to conceive a child who would experience inherited emotions like anxiety, depression, and PTSD.

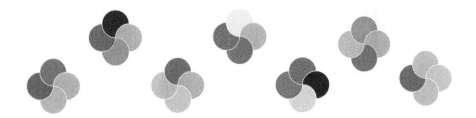

Inherited family trauma is not a popular case in our society and so victims of this receive little to know help in dealing with the trauma. Therapy and medications may offer temporary relief, but nothing offers a lasting treatment if the cause is not identified, which is what is being sought after. There isn't many research on A solution that offers an explanation and lasting result on these, so the knowledge on this is limited.

Generational trauma occurs when traumatic experiences of the previous generations are transferred from one generation to another. This idea of generational trauma was first revealed by Canadian psychiatrist *Vivian M. Take-off, MD*, and her colleagues in 1966. They recorded a high number of psychological distresses among children of Holocaust survivors. The grandchildren of Holocaust survivors were overrepresented by about 300% in psychiatric care referrals. This was established in a study called "*The Canadian Journal of Psychiatry.*" As a result, Holocaust survivors and their progeny have been the most widely studied groups. However, in theory, extreme prolonged stress of any type can have adverse psychological effects on children and grandchildren, leading to clinical anxiety, depression, and post-traumatic stress disorder (PTSD).

When you experience an inherited trauma, there are usually physical and emotional reactions. Examples of such reactions may include trouble sleeping, anxiety, feeling disconnected or confused, having intrusive thoughts, withdrawing from others, etc. depending on how severe the effects were. However, in children and growing adolescence, this can look like tummy aches, problems sleeping, attempting to avoid school, overeating, uncontrollable anger, fear, or showing attention-seeking behaviours, etc.

That was the case with Rachael. After years of taking antidepressants, attending talk and group therapy, and trying various cognitive approaches to mitigate the effects of stress, her symptoms of depression and anxiety remained unchanged. She always sees herself getting overwhelmed by the littlest stress or overreacting when exposed to little risk. It was as if she was being triggered unconsciously from a realm beyond her control. The therapeutic sessions and talks were not helpful, as most of the things said were not entirely applicable to

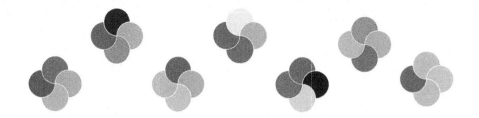

her. Her case was different. She knew something was not right, yet she didn't know where to get the solutions and help she desired.

Somehow, she was invited for a session on inherited family trauma. At first, she waved it off as a psychological disorder common to only holocaust survivors or those affected by severe effects, such as slave trades, war, or famine. She tried to minimise it, not knowing that the topic was entirely relatable to her. Somehow, she attended the session and listened faintly during the meeting, one ear with an earbud listening to hip-hop while the other partially listening to the teachings.

It started becoming interesting when the term inherited family trauma was first explained, instances given, and the effects recalled. Her eyes broadened, her mouth almost wide opened, and she felt that somehow God brought her to the right source even after having so many doubts about it. At that instance, she jumped to her feet, grabbed a note, and paid more attention. From the stage where I stood, I could sense a change in her attitude, even though I didn't know her intention. Hence, I picked interest. I broadly explained the topic, and before the session ended, Rachael had a couple of notes. She asked several questions, using herself as a case study.

Right after the meeting, Rachael picked the form and booked an appointment. I was happy to see her. During the session, I realized how much she has suffered from carrying the emotions of her previous generations. During the conversation, she told me she no longer wanted to live. For as long as she could remember, she had struggled with emotions so intense she could barely suppress the urges in her body. Rachael had been admitted severally to a psychiatric hospital, where she was diagnosed as bipolar with a severe anxiety disorder. Medication brought her slight relief but never touched the powerful suicidal urges that lived inside her. As a teenager, she would self-harm by burning herself with a lighter or iron just to feel pain. Now, at twenty-eight, Rachael has had enough. Her depression and anxiety, which she said, have prevented her from being in a relationship or focusing on her job to achieve results deserving of promotions.

Rachael knew the basic of her family history, but she had never connected it to her anxiety and depression. While we traced down her family genogram, identifying the plausible stories and pains of the previous generations, we came across a striking one. Her grandmother's elder sister was raped few days before her wedding. This made her extremely depressed. She couldn't control it. She committed suicide and passed on before the wedding was even conducted. This effect sent an impulse of fear to the family, few years later they moved on, and the story buried, yet its effect was visible to the family members.

"Alas, we found it, there it is", I exclaimed. The fear and anxiety of your grandmother has passed on to you yet unconsciously, and its effect manifesting severely. She was counseled and given several assignments. Most of the counsels, exercises, daily habits given to her are also written and compiled and are found in this workbook.

In the same way, you inherit your parent's blood type, physical looks, hair color, height, etc., so do certain genes responsible for the documentation of their traumatic experiences transfer to you, which makes you behave and reason just like them. Family trauma is inheritable the way genes and physical features are inherited from parents—Anxiety, unhappiness, troubled relationships, and depression can also be inherited without the individual even knowing.

Before now Scientists used to dismiss non-coding DNA (ncDNA) as "junk DNA," believing it to be ineffective, but they've recently discovered its use. scientists having a better knowledge of the human genome discovered that chromosomal DNA—the DNA responsible for conveying physical features like hair, eyes, and skin colour—makes up less than 2% of your total DNA. The remaining 98 percent is non-coding DNA (ncDNA), responsible for many of our emotional, behavioural, and personality characteristics.

To eliminate the generational effects of family trauma, parents or affected individuals need to access their family's history or possibly ask relatives about their family's past. Such questions can help redirect their focus away from the current effects and toward the source, assisting them in discovering a potential

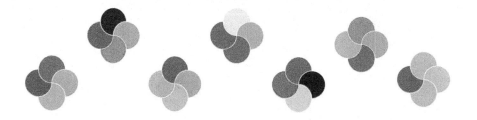

cure for overcoming this trauma and being completely free. Most of the time, these questions may appear basic and not too necessary.

If my grandparents jumped from one relationship to the other, Or they suffered from obesity, depression, even tried to commit suicide? what was the cause? Was is an inherited trauma or a possible traumatic experience.

UNDERSTANDING THESE TRAUMATIC BEHAVIOURS

In the 18th century, some groups of researchers used the mice study to simplify these traumatic behaviors. During the research, the parent mice were exposed to high-level risks and careful psychological monitoring to ensure that they experienced trauma to a large degree. Some strange behaviors happened to the mice who had experienced traumatic conditions before the experiment. they began behaving in a depressive way, others started losing their natural aversion to bright lights and open spaces. These visible behaviors were transmitted from one offspring to another. Through thorough observation, it was discovered that stress related to traumatic events changed the amount of microRNA in the biological makeup of the offspring mice. They discovered an increased amount of microRNA in the traumatized mice and a lower amount in the average mice. Within the offspring of the mice who had experienced or inherited these traumas, the insulin and blood sugar were much lower than the offspring of the average mice. This finding was of great importance to the researchers as it served as major evidence — traumatic experiences can affect the metabolism and behaviors of both humans and most animals.

Jacob Peterson, a prominent member of the legislative arm of the state government, always has anger issues that affected his judgment and emotional state. during a legislative meeting, he usually sees his emotions prevailing over his decisions. He has struggled with this issue and attended many anger management classes, but nothing seemed to work. Luckily, he came across the subject's inherited family trauma and attended a

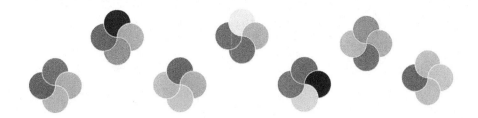

therapeutic session where the subject was explained to him. Also, proper follow-ups and training sessions were administered, and in due time, he could get his emotions on the track and in check. He no longer overreacted at little provocations or flared up when involved in a brief argument. He gained full mastery of his emotions and could apply the prior knowledge he had more effectively.

Most of you are like Jacob, struggling with an inherited emotion maybe addiction, anger, fear, or anxiety, and find yourself unable to apply the things being taught from other therapeutic sessions, or maybe you've tried, and yet nothing seems to work. The good news is that your recovery is guaranteed once you're able to figure out the cause of your emotions by tracking them down to your **family history.**

It's important to understand that the traumatic experience you have is natural. The fears, the shyness, timidity, or overwhelming emotions like anxiety, unexplained phobias, anger, etc, are all natural and might have been passed down to you. And are not necessarily yours. Why don't you return it? Why don't you let it go? Why don't you embrace the real you? A transformed being freed from the burdens of your fore generations. This book is a masterpiece in highlighting these inherited emotions and overcoming them.

IDENTIFYING INHERITED FAMILY TRAUMA

Statistics show that 60% of men and 50% of women experience at least one traumatic event during their lifetime. Over the years, I have seen people with traumatizing emotions wave it off by attributing the cause to other factors. One time, a married man, Mr. Cameron, had this fear of being abandoned by his wife and starting all over? The fear was so severe that it resulted in controlling and constantly checking up on his wife. His excuse was that growing up, he was always abandoned and his heart broken, he never

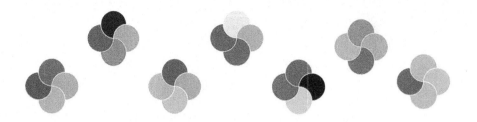

sustained a relationship. He feared his wife would be like his several breakups.

To him, his fear resulted from the several past encounters he had. Little did he know that his encounters and fears were all traced to the inherited emotions and trauma of his fore generation. Identifying these traumas most times requires a deepened level of mindfulness and an understanding of your family history.

What symptoms do I have?

In this section, we would first examine ourselves to identify some traumatic symptoms affecting our daily lives and activities. Give yourself 10points for every correct answer. If you don't relate with any, go ahead in the box below and describe the symptoms you feel.

1. Anger; are you easily provoked and angry about little things, or are you struggling with emotional outbursts, hatred, or anger?

    YES   NO

2. Nightmares; how are you sleeping? Do you see yourself dreaming about things that may never happen, or will never happen? Are your dreams frightening or always occurring?

    YES   NO

3. Lack of trust in others. Do you find it difficult trusting others and yourself (abilities, talents,) etc.

    YES   NO

4. Fearfulness, irritability; are you afraid of almost everything, or you're easily irritable.

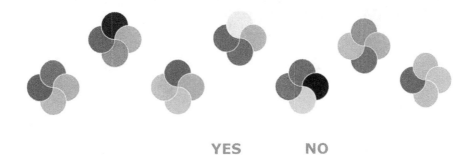

YES   NO

5. Inability to connect with others. How are your relationships with others? Do you find it difficult socializing, or do you cover up with claims of being introverted.

YES   NO

ARE THERE MORE? WRITE IT IN THE BOX BELOW

_____

_____

_____

_____

_____

_____

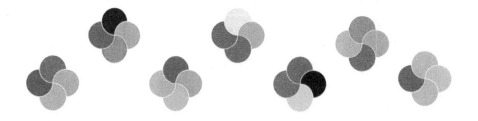

Are there more symptoms?

This section is a continuation of the previous. In this section, you're presented with different symptoms where trauma may have manifested in you. Tick the correct option if such a condition applies to you.

Physical signs

- Constant worry and complaints about the littlest of things

    TRUE   FALSE

- Unusual bodily feelings

    TRUE   FALSE

- Overwhelming emotions, and reactions at benign remarks and words, most times your perspective is extremely different from the supposed

    TRUE   FALSE

Emotional Changes

- Being hypersensitive to emotional content (movies, songs, books, etc

    TRUE   FALSE

- Feeling disconnected from your emotions and your body

    TRUE   FALSE

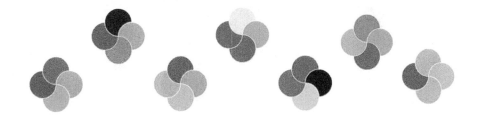

- Feeling helpless or hopeless about the future

  TRUE   FALSE

- Being constantly angry or irritated at people and their actions

  TRUE   FALSE

- Being constantly cynical or jumping to conclusions

  TRUE   FALSE

Traumatic Behaviours

- Most times, you unconsciously avoid going to work or planned events, even when there is no reason

  TRUE   FALSE

- At a point in your life, you lost interest in activities that used to give you joy, like sports, watching movies, or other hobbies

  TRUE   FALSE

- You notice changes in your relationships, like people avoiding you or you avoiding others

  TRUE   FALSE

- Sooner than later, you have difficulty relating with others

  TRUE   FALSE

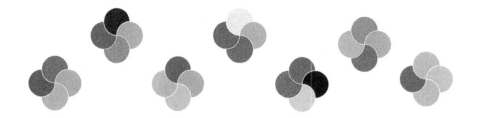

- Small talk becomes meaningless and difficult to relate with

    TRUE   FALSE

- You believe no one understands you

    TRUE   FALSE

- Isolating yourself completely from others or only interacting with people who are in your same immediate environment, most times very few

    TRUE   FALSE

IDENTIFY YOUR COPING SKILLS,

Most times, the inherited trauma manifests through your coping skills. Most people try to suppress their traumatic effects. They try to numb it down either by drinking, cooling off, or pretending it never happened.

For the traumatic experience mentioned above, what coping mechanism did you adopt for it? Tick to the ones that relate to you. Are there more? Write them down in the space below.

- Criticising yourself for almost everything
- Chewing your fingernails
- Becoming aggressive or violent (hitting someone, throwing, or kicking Something
- Eating too much or too little or drinking a lot of coffee

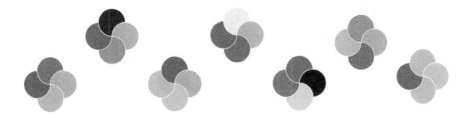

- Smoking or chewing tobacco
- Drinking alcohol

Are there more? Write them below.

1. _____

2. _____

3. _____

4. _____

5. _____

SCHOOL ON FAMILY HISTORY.

To identify an inherited family trauma, you must commit to "school on family history." You study, talk, interview, and ask questions until you have all the information you need to assess and understand the root of inherited family trauma.

KNOWING WHAT YOU WANT

The aim of this book is solely to enable you to become a better individual with stable emotions and better control over your response and reaction. But you must figure out what you want and walk with it, Set out time each day, go through the exercises in this book, ensure to read the book till the end and take note where necessary, highlight main paragraphs and do all that is instructed of you. Doing this puts you at a greater advantage of overcoming

inherited family trauma and experiencing life to the fullest. Knowing what you want can help you live a healthy and stable life.

In knowing what you want, you acknowledge that:

1. *That you are willing to heal;* your belief must match your expectations. You must accept and be willing to heal, you must say no to the former pattern of feeling and reasoning, and be ready to embark on your recovery.

2. *You need and should accept support from others:* When you are healing from trauma, you must establish a connection with others regularly and avoid isolating yourself. You must surround yourself with people who love, respect, and support you. People who are invaluable to your healing process.

3. *That you need the help of professionals:* The issues of trauma may not be treated solely by glaring through the laptop screen or flipping through the pages of a book, yes this may help, but at most times, it is helpful to seek professional training from a certified therapist.

4. *That you need to incorporate movement and proper exercises in your daily routine:* As a part of healing, though not mandatory, it is helpful that you exercise more frequently. Doing this causes oxygen to flow to the brain, hence triggering the rate of healing. Also, physical activities like yoga and meditation make you feel safe and stable.

DENIAL AND MINIMISATION

Unidentified trauma is hidden in minimised emotions and denied pain. Most individuals struggle with the inability to identify their suffering as it relates to an inherited experience. Most times, they assume it to be stress or because of their environment, parents, or even basic needs like clothing, accessories, etc. You hear them give excuses for their emotional outbursts, anxiety, anger, etc,

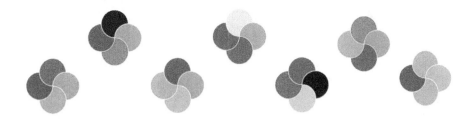

attributing its causes to a person, place, or thing. My husband is so stubborn he doesn't listen to me when, in sincerity, their anxiety is taking greater hold of them. Below is a story of one of my clients who struggled with anger:

Joseph Wilberforce shared a room with a colleague while studying for his master's program. though he wasn't comfortable, he managed it because he had no option. Moreover, he was limited in funds and refused to take money from his siblings and parents. He struggled with one thing 'anger.' when confronted, he denied and claimed to be a cheerful person and that anger was not part of him. He claimed that while growing up, no one ever complained of his uncontrollable emotions and that he was known as the cheerful kid on the block. Little did he know that the inherited anger was part of his recessive genes, thus preventing the immediate manifestation of these emotions.

It soon became a problem, not just to him, but to those around him. People withdrew from him. His friends soon avoided him. Before he could realize a potential flaw that needed reckoning, a series of damage had been done. It took him time and boldness to accept anger as a weakness and the need to deal with it.

He was never born with it. In fact, throughout his high school and university days, he never experienced anger, not knowing anger was embedded in his genes and would manifest later in his life. During therapy with a professional, he was brought to light on inherited family trauma, from which the cause of his anger manifesting at a later age was discovered and treatment rendered.

Minimizing and denying the effect of an inherited trauma is more common in individuals than you might expect. You may try to minimize extremely traumatic events that continue to affect you long after the event has passed, but you can never overcome the effects of inherited family trauma by denying or minimizing the effect. You can't keep claiming you're the cheerful type when in reality, there are traces of unexplained sadness, depression, etc. Check yourself. How do you feel? Accept it, then aim to overcome it by ensuring you follow the instructions as specified by a therapist or a professional workbook.

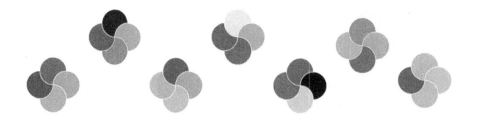

Until you admit the truth to yourself, you will not progress on your recovery path.

RECORD YOURSELF

In this section, you are expected to record your activities, reactions, and daily experiences in 7 weeks or a 2-month time frame, remember for your healing to be effective, it needs to be done right. This section might take time. You can answer the exercises for today, come back some other day, and continue, remember to put an indicator or book separator or if you're reading from kindle, or as an eBook do well to bookmark this page for future consulting and references.

The aim of doing this is to understand the emotions that manifest themselves the most. It is an effective strategy for knowing and separating the inherited trauma from obvious bodily reactions.

To be on the safer side, it is beneficial that you print out copies of these pages and keep a record of them, or get a journal that would help you keep track. It is recommended that you keep an account of your progress by doing this as a group or with your partner, friends, etc.

How to heal from generational trauma?

While Jacob struggled with the overwhelming emotions of anger and depression, he came across the of inherited family trauma, after which his life was transformed. For most people, the topic might be new to them, while for others, they have been having struggle on recovery for a long time. The good news is that you will overcome these emotions if you carefully and strictly follow the instructions in these books. The exercises, the daily practices, etc.

Healing from inherited family trauma requires a series of processes if it is to be successful and effective. Most of this process will be highlighted in the next chapters as you keep reading and working with us.

CHAPTER TWO

Retracing the Origin Of Inherited Family Trauma

We often have common characteristics with members of our family. It might be you talk like your grandmother; you walk like your uncle; you have your mother's eyes, your father's long legs, your grandfather's smile, hair colour, skin tone, etc. All these are inherited characteristics that have been genetically passed down generation after generation. But just like these attributes can be inherited, Without our conscious efforts in changing the pattern. it may linger to our unborn child.

A terrible situation that might have occurred a hundred years can cause its effect to reoccur in an offspring causing an in-explainable trauma response. Trauma is usually visible in actions and words and this is the reason it is advised to pay close attention to what the victim says [core complaint, descriptions etc] as this might give you pointers to the origin of this problem.

According to Thomas Verny, "the experience in the womb moulds the brain and provides the framework underlying your character, emotional temperament, and the potential of cognitive reasoning". These patterns are passed along more than learned, much like a blueprint.

When dealing with patients that suffers from depression, anxiety or any other mental health issue, it is important to look back into the family history at least three generations back, record any major event that might have taken place in the lives of the ancestors and how it may have affected their lives, the lives of the children and grandchildren alike. Also, proper research needs to be carried out to identify if another member of the family might have also inherited this trauma or may show signs of this trauma.

It is the human nature to feel pain, despair, frustration or regret, but when it gets too much, it is also the human nature to avoid these feelings and try to suppress it. This doesn't take away the pain or the feelings, but carefully hides it for a long period. However, this pain would seek outlets to be expressed. A pathway to emerge and these pathways could be visible in the next generation who do not know the origin of the pain. When pain is avoided, it often protracts, which is the exact opposite of what you try to achieve by avoiding it.

in the previous chapters we identified the source of inherited family trauma to stem from our parents and fore generations, we got to understand the scientific discovery on the origin of trauma and how its effect persists in the behaviour and experiences of an individual even after several years.

In this chapter, we would be more focused on retracing the origin of these inherited traumas, how to unravel the events they experienced, and access the same sensation they once felt. We will also address how to ask the right questions in getting answers to the traumatic experience which are most times buried with family history.

One thing is sure, at the end of this session you will unravel the past, dig into your family history and, most important understand the root course of your traumatic behaviours and inherited emotions.

In this chapter, we would retrace the origin of this trauma and best ways to overcome and avoid it.

TO GO FORWARD TAKE A LOOK BACKWARD

Trauma is an emotional response to a terrible event a person encountered. This doesn't mean a person has to be present in order to get traumatised, as terrible events can take different forms, and this doesn't make it any less traumatising. These emotions are registered in your brain and fragments of these memories are dispersed as images, sounds, body movements or words and are stored in your subconscious which can be triggered by anything

remotely related to the original event. This explains why victims of inherited trauma can go about their normal life for a long period with no trace of any problem till an event trigger this long buried emotion and the victims experience inherited emotions.

Something victims of inherited family trauma have in common, apart from inheriting feelings, is the confusion that comes right after. When you experience a sudden burst of emotions that you can't explain, it's normal to think "it'll just go away with time" and when it doesn't, you source for solutions and explanations to why you feel that way. Often, you look inwards at your life — incidents that you might have experienced, moments that might have made you sad, or anything just to give a reason or an explanation for your feelings. You go to therapy, take medications and when these fail, you're left in a state of total confusion 'what led you down this path?'.

This might pose as a problem as victims of inherited trauma do not know the trauma, they suffer isn't theirs and, most times, they have little to no knowledge of members of the family that might have suffered the same faith and so cannot connect the dots. For this reason, it is very important to always look back into your family history and keep a record of events or situations that might have traumatised members of your family. At the end of these chapter are guidelines for unveiling the traumatic events in your family history. most important, enabling you to overcome the challenges that come with living with these traumas.

Making peace with your family history.

Most inherited trauma starts with our parents trying to suppress the pains or emotional trauma they experienced, doing so unknowingly stunts the healing process that should have led to a natural release. Most times they think The less a child knows, the better for the child, as it would protect the child from feeling bad, contrary to their thoughts the pain submerge into their genetic, until it finds a pathway for expression and manifest themselves generations later.

Making peace with your family history starts with knowing and experiencing the same emotions they might have experienced and releasing it in proper ways; it is reconnecting the link back to them, putting yourself in their shoes and expressing it more adequately. Giving them that soothing comfort and reassurance of being with them.

Most times, making peace with your family history could involve identifying the stresses they experienced, relating it with your presence circumstance and making amends where necessary. This doesn't mean you have to experience the event they did, but being that link to re comfort, express and accept these emotions. Only then can you suppress these inherited feelings. Only then can you break the link between the past and your present self.

Having direct access to these sensations,

In this section, you are required to create a direct connection to your family's traumatic events. In doing these we are trying to experience their emotions and consoling them where necessary. This section is further divided into different components.

First is to write out your present experiences. What are those hidden emotions that have been submerged in your body? Deal with them first.

This present moment, here and now, if you're to describe how you feel, what would it be? Write it in the space provided below.

_____

_____

_____

_____

_____

_____

_____

_____

What inherited feeling do you think you have? List them all out, and you keep reading. You can come back to edit the list and refocusing it to the core inherited trauma.

_____

_____

_____

_____

_____

_____

_____

_____

Do your friends complain about your attitude? If yes, what are these complaints? Write as much as you can remember?

_____

_____

_____

_____

_____

_____

_____

From the list above, describe an event that made you feel this way? It could be a normal event or even a traumatising event. Whatever the event is, write them out. If you can't recall any event at all, please move over to the next session. You can always come back to fill this list.

_____

_____

_____

_____

core languages and sentences

Your core languages are the unconscious words you say when faced with difficulty of any kind. They are good pointers on realising a traumatic

experience from family history. They as well are good indicators in identifying inherited emotions from a traumatic experience in a family history.

In most cases they go beyond the verbal word you say, they could as well be the words you are writing, the critic you give to yourself without saying it out loud could also be a notable indicator to unveiling the origin of your inherited emotions, characters and thinking patterns.

Most core sentences from victims of inherited trauma are usually negative and self-condemning. They are accompanied with a personalisation — an address as though they own the thoughts. They begin with pronouns such as "I, we, they, me"

some common core languages that resonate in the average victims of inherited trauma include the following

"I am not good enough,"

"Nobody wants me,"

"They are going to destroy me. "

"They hate me,"

They will kill me. "

"I blame myself,"

"it's my fault,"

"I'm tired of living,"

"The world isn't safe for me. "

"I hate myself,"

To get the best out of a recurring core language, it is helpful that we implore the use of Bridging questions. Bridging questions are questions that create a link between the core language and an experience from family history, most of which existed or occurred before you were born.

Notable symptoms of core sentence

- Whenever you utter a core sentence, you experience physical and emotional reactions like fear. Anxiety, anger, etc.
- Core sentence are indicators of an unresolved tragedy
- Core sentences affect the way your body and mind functions
- It disrupts the joy, happiness and peace of mind you might have been experiencing before the core languages sprang up
- Core languages, when spoken, worsen our emotional state
- Core languages make situations seem more complicated than they are

some Questions That Generate Core Language

1. When your symptom or problem first appeared, what was going on in your life
2. What happened just before it started
3. When the symptom or problem first appeared, what age were you
4. Did someone in your family go through a traumatic experience at a similar age?
5. Describe the problem
6. How does it feel when it's at its worst?
7. What occurs immediately before you feel this way or experience the symptom
8. What provokes it to improve or deteriorate
9. What is the problem or symptom preventing you from doing? What are you compelled to do because of it?
10. What would be the worst thing that could happen to you if the feeling or symptom never went away

Using Your core Language as pointers

Inherited trauma most times are expressed in your languages. What you say could be a link to a family history once affected by trauma. For most victim core languages could be the trigger for uncovering the buried history in your family history.

You can use the following questions to discover your core language. You should answer each. Make sure your responses are open and honest.

A. At the time your problem or symptom first appeared, what were you experiencing in your life
B. Approximately what age were you when the symptoms or problems first appeared
C. Did someone in your family go through something traumatic at the same age as you?
D. When the trauma occurs, what does it exactly do? Describe its effect on you.
E. When it is at its worst, how does it make you feel
F. In the moments, leading up to feeling this way or experiencing the symptom, what happens
G. Are there any differences or improvements?
H. How does the problem or symptom hinder your ability to operate? What do you find yourself forced to do as a result?
I. Could you imagine anything that would be worse if the feeling or symptom never faded.

Using your Core complaints as pointers

Complaints generally are reactions when treated unfairly. Oxford language dictionary defined it as a statement that something is unsatisfactory or unacceptable. Core complaints are imprints of unsatisfied or unacceptable events most of which may be traumatic, that may have happened to our

fore fathers. These imprints resonate a series of complaint and overwhelming emotions In the offspring.

Besides providing healing for inherited trauma that has never fully resolved, complaints can also illuminate a personal guilt we carry [most times imprinted in our DNA], perhaps even pointing the way to reconciliation.

Whatever may cause your trauma, there are core complaints attached to your core language. We all harbour a fear that something will happen to us in the future. We reveal this fear in our core complaints.

Example of core complaints

"Life is hard",

"I'm a walking dead".

"I'm tired of living",

"Everybody hates me",

"I don't have strength",

"I don't have…" etc

To investigate your core complaints, get a **pen** and **paper** or a **notebook** and answer the following questions sincerely.

Take the following exercise In identifying your major core complaints:
1. Focus solely on a problem that is currently the most pressing in your life. It could be a problem with your health, your job, or your relationship—anything that makes you feel unsafe, uneasy, or unwell.

2. What is the most serious issue you'd like to resolve? Perhaps it's a problem that feels intractable. You may find it overwhelming. Maybe it's a symptom or a sensation you've had for a long time. It's your life. List them out.

3. What would you like to see change?

4. Make a list of what is important to you.

5. As it occurs to you, write it down. You might, for example, have a fear of something bad is going to happen to you in the future. It makes no difference. Just keep writing until it comes out.

6. If nothing appears, respond to the following question: If the sensation, symptom, or What would you be afraid could happen if the condition you have never goes away? Is this something that has happened to you

Don't read any further until you've written your most pressing concerns.

_____

_____

_____

_____

_____

_____

Core descriptors

There are many painful images in our lives; images of our parents not providing enough for us or even images of not getting what we needed from them. If left unchecked, these images control the course of our lives.

Descriptors allow you gain insight on the inherited feelings of fore parents who were victims of trauma. They reveal feelings you didn't even realise you had. They are sentences expressed when describing a person. Using core descriptors gives room for expression which may be hidden. When you describe a person or event, your mind is channelled into a state of subconscious, this state gives you room for actual reasoning and deep thinking which provides full expression of the person you are describing.

Core descriptors is an expression of your feelings. The feelings once concealed in our blood. Most times it is an expression of the body suffering either inherited or in the present. When you give a description about a person especially you are unravelling the emotions attached towards the person. If I'm giving a description about my mom, my description would not only address the good side, it will as well describe the faults, from a perspective of being offended

In this session, we would describe our family, starting with our fathers and mothers. We can as well extend it to an extended family, uncle aunty etc. those that shares same filial generation with our parents. Most times your description of your family, both extended and nuclear, could hold significant behavioural patterns helpful in unveiling hidden traumatic experience in your family history.

Describing Your Mother

In the comments and space given below, describe your mother. What don't you like about her? Highlight the consequences, the flaws, the notable signs or even

the intriguing emotions. Also, write what you blame her for. Write as much characteristics as you can remember, you can even write out the events that made you conclude these.

Some common core descriptors include;

- "Mom seemed distant." She never hugged me in her arms. "I had no faith in her.
- "My mother was too preoccupied to care for me." She didn't have time for me.
- "My mother and I have a really close relationship. She's like my little sister, whom I look after.
- "I don't want to ever be a bother to my mother.
- "My mother was critical, aloof, and emotionally inaccessible.
- "She always pushed me away." She seems unconcerned about me.
- "We don't actually have a relationship.
- "I felt a lot more connected to my grandmother." She was the one who • gave birth to me.
- "My mum is very self-absorbed." Everything revolves around her. She had showed no affection for me…
- "She has a knack for calculating and manipulating people." With her, I didn't feel protected.
- "I was terrified of her." "I was never sure what would happen next
- "I don't have a good relationship with her." She isn't a mother.
- "I've never been interested in having children." "I've never felt maternal within.

"Now it's your turn. In the comment below, describe your mother.

My mother was… I blame my mother for…

Describing Your Father

Same way you described your mother, say a word or two about your father, what do you hate the most, what notable signs could be associated with an inherited trauma.

For example, *my father was a drunk, an addict to gambling. He spent most of his time either in the bear parlour or in a casino wasting away. He never had time for me or the family. Growing up, I rarely noticed his absence.*

Now is your turn. Describe your father

My father was . . .. I blame my father for . . .

_____

_____

_____

_____

_____

_____

_____

_____

_____

_____

_____

Describing Your external family, Partner, Close Friend, or boss.

For most traumatic cases especially cases of slave trade, kidnap, death, and sexual abuse may not only affect the victim but may leave imprints in the siblings of the victims. These imprints also manifest in their offspring and their lives.

Describing your extended relations and family could provide clues on a buried family history. Mark wolynn, in one of his bestselling *book* **it didn't start with you,** describes these descriptors as a doorway into our unconscious feelings. Which can reveal feelings about your parents' immediate family that you might not even be aware of.

In the section below, describe any of your relation uncles, aunties even cousins. The aim is to identify resonating symptoms of inherited emotions. You can broaden the search to their childhood friends, business patners etc. those that were with them from childhood.

My aunt/uncle, partner, close friend, or boss is. . I blame him/her for.

_____

_____

_____

_____

_____

_____

_____

_____

_____

Traceable signs to watch out for,

Your emotions are guidelines in highlighting your core languages. The emotional charge in your core descriptors can function like a barometer to gauge the healing that still needs to take place. The stronger the negative charge, the clearer the direction for healing. You are looking for words that contain a significant emotional charge. When you say most of the words from above, how do you feel inwardly? Beyond the feeling of anger and hate lies traces of an inherited emotion.

Nene had always hated marriage. On the surface, she claimed to be a feminist and sexist of the woman gender. She gets angry and topples anyone that tries to talk her into marriage or even relationship; she claimed all these were bonds the society used to cripple the woman's strength. Beyond her irrational belief and understanding lies a fear. Nene's greatest fear was giving birth. She always thought of dying in the process and hated anything that would lead to such incidence. The underlining signal for nene wasn't the hatred for the male gender, but the fear of falling in love and dying during childbirth. Nene fear for pregnancy was so severe that it affected her body structure and she experienced heightened pain during menstruation.

Having known her core complaint, and underlying emotions she was able to unfold series of event that happened to her grandmother, at fourteen her grandmother was kidnapped and sold off during the slave trade that occurred in Nigeria, while they journeyed, few kilometres from the shores they celebrated their loots with drinks and lots of merry, in the course of their highness and celebration they took turns on her, and she bled to death. Her body was disposed into the river and it floated ashore close to home. The results sent unwavering shocks to the members of the family, and mentioning it became a taboo. Even

after slave trade was abolished and the era of industrialisation took over, this traumatising events continued to unborn generations though its severity reduced.

An exercise for you; Go back to your core descriptions of your parents, then follow the exercises that follow.

1. Go over your core descriptors once again. This time around Read them aloud and slowly.
2. While reading, Listen from a variety of perspective. Is there anything new that you've heard? Do you have any other sensations?
3. While reading, if you noticed yourself having any emotion then the emotion driven words imply that you still harbor resentment toward your parents.
4. As you read the descriptors, feel your body. Is your body tense or relaxed? What about your inhalation? Is it moving or is it stuck? what other body sensory do you notice.
5. Check to see if anything inside you wants to change.

Some core themes that repeat itself in families

The following themes are common with people struggling with inherited trauma,
- repetitions of core languages,
- repetitions of ages,
- repetitions of behaviours, symptoms and emotions etc.

in this section we will look at these notable repetitions relating them as clues to uncovering your inherited emotions, traumas and behaviours.

Repetition of languages

From your core languages, we could unearth some possible repeated trauma languages; we could identify most of these languages as it relates to

inherited traumas. In the life of every victimized family of trauma lies a language traceable to the painful experiences of their fore generations.

I am not good enough; I've lost it all. Laura would always say to herself, maybe she is right or maybe it's an inherited trauma language, let's figure these out.

Laura was a successful athlete, usually the best in most indoor sporting activities, in 2019 she was the overall best in judo and second runner in the state table tennis competition, she was the pride of her school and everybody speculated she might turn out winner in the forthcoming national table tennis competition. She was ready, but underneath her experiences lies a traumatic inheritance.

Her grandfather at an early age had a self-esteem problem associated with a series of abuse he experienced while staying with his foster parents. The trauma resonated in the lives of Laura and sooner than expected the once energetic damsel started losing her touch, her esteem weakened, and her confidence diminished, soon she started dropping and completely lost her abilities, reason not that she can't do it but an unexplained fear, anxiety and frustration gripped her, she couldn't even perform like she used to. Her school employed most therapist to handle her case, but every prescription was like pouring water in the basket. How do you figure out a problem, when everything seems normal from the surface?

When she was exposed to the subject of inherited trauma through the help of an external consultant, she realized connection with the sufferings and emotions of her grandfather. Her core language being a major factor in her realization.

I'm not good enough being the resonated insults and abuse the grandfather received which affected his esteem and made him see himself as not good enough

I've lost it all being are words born out of regrets of her grandfather at a later age, on realizing his esteem has wrecked his life, the opportunities he failed to embrace and much more the life he once wished he could have which turned out to be an impossible case as age was already at his doorstep.

From the previous sections, we have dealt with your core languages as a sign of an inherited trauma. Perhaps you didn't fully express yourself. In the section below, are there some languages you say when you're angry, sad, frustrated or ignored, list them out If you can remember. If not, take out time to monitor your activities for a day or a week, you can as well get an activity logbook to record the emotions

Some noticeable core language I usually repeat are

1.
_____

2.
_____

3.
_____

4.
_____

5.
_____

6.
_____

Repetition of ages

Most inherited trauma are traceable to the ages at which they once occurred. A grand mom who was abused at age 19 might find the same

traumatic emotions resonating in the lives of her grandchild at same age. Most traumas that resonate in the life of its victims, mostly, occur at the same age at which their grandparents were abused. Although, in most cases, age doesn't hold the entire reason for its reoccurrence. To most others, like Nancy, age was a negligible factor. Her grandfather's regrets manifested at a later age, older than the age Laura was when hers started resonating.

To curb the effect of this trauma, it is important that you relate your present predicament to the age at which a traumatic experienced might have occurred. Figure out if you were the same age as someone in your family when their problem or symptom first occurred?

At what age did you start experiencing the unexplainable emotions?

_____

Describe these emotions you believe to be an inherited trauma

_____

_____

_____

_____

_____

_____

_____

Are there any story from your grandparents or parents that resonates with the age written above? If there is write them down below. If none, take a day or two to ask questions where necessary.

Some questions to ask has already been provided below. Here is more to ask in getting answers.

1. Did anything happen to my parent or grandparent at age 13, or from age 13 to 29, replace 13 with the ages at which your traumatic experience occurred? If you're not sure, then replace 13 and 29 with the age range you remember. In the space below, write out the traumatic experience.

I.e. *What happened to my mother at 17 or from age 16 to 19. What happened to my father at age 20, or probably age 20 to 39. etc*

Note; Always relate it with your present age, traumatic emotions and feelings.

_____

_____

_____

_____

_____

Repetition of behaviors, symptoms and emotions

Your behaviours, symptoms and emotions are good indicator of an inherited trauma, that may have resonated. For most people with hostile behaviours and anger issue, their inherited trauma may be associated with a history of abuse, suffering or excessive inconvenience. These emotions which are suppressed later manifest in the offspring and third filial generations as compulsive behaviours and overwhelming emotions

Taking a flashback to the early stage of your trauma. Do you remember when its symptoms started manifesting? What was the trigger, what happening behind the scenes? Did someone leave you? Did you feel rejected or abandoned? Is your issue or symptom related to anything that happened to you in your childhood? Is it similar to anything you witnessed or experienced while growing up? Did any event happen to your mother, father, grandmother, grandfather, or great-grandparents? Most times these events are triggers to our inherited emotions and could be clue for identifying inherited trauma.

The answers to these questions will help in revealing the root cause of your inherited trauma.

Connecting the dots back to your parents

Your parent are the first link of an inherited trauma. Most times they are the benefactor of the traumatic experience. They are witnesses to event that might have happened or been told. When seeking explanation to these trauma it Is necessary that you connect the dots back to your parent. Start from your parents, what do they know, what happened to them at particular age, how is their behaviours and reactions, what changed about them from early childhood till now, what are their core complaints, descriptors and languages. these informations would uncorver the once buried family history.

In this session, we will look at your parent's history, also connect every similar characteristic with our present selves

Your parents' history, what can you remember

Among the stories your parents ever told you, are there any that made you feel pity for them? Write out this story in the space below or in your journal if you can remember any of them. If not, please move to the next question.

_____

_____

_____

_____

_____

_____

Aside from the story written, what significant event happened in their childhood? Was any member of their family harmed, murdered, or even taken advantage of? If yes, what was the story of the harm? What really happened to them? Or to their families?

_____

_____

_____

_____

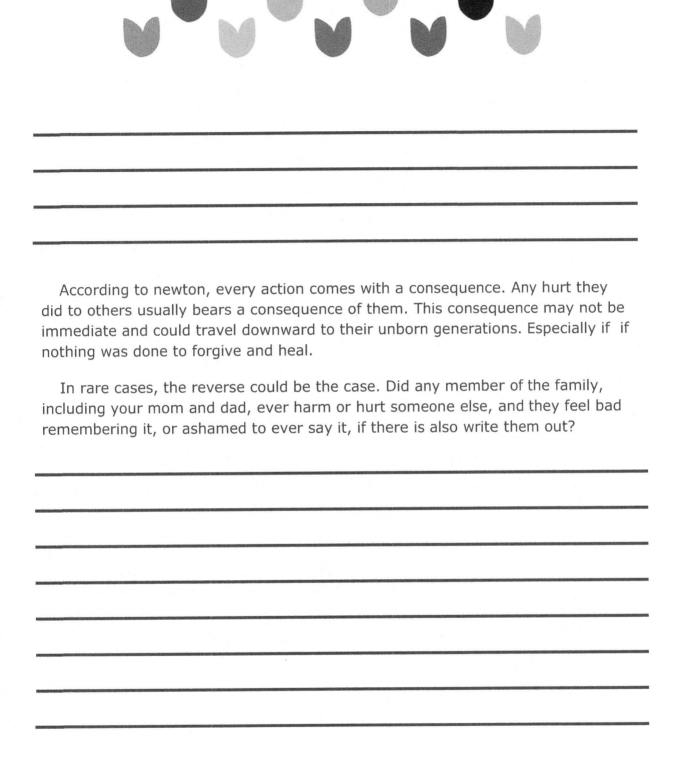

According to newton, every action comes with a consequence. Any hurt they did to others usually bears a consequence of them. This consequence may not be immediate and could travel downward to their unborn generations. Especially if if nothing was done to forgive and heal.

In rare cases, the reverse could be the case. Did any member of the family, including your mom and dad, ever harm or hurt someone else, and they feel bad remembering it, or ashamed to ever say it, if there is also write them out?

Connect your present age with their own experience

The traumatising event you experience, have they been like that since childhood? If the answer is no, then answer the question, but if your answer is yes, then move on to the next session. In rare cases, it might be an infant transgenerational problem. what happened when they were your age?

1. **Describe your childhood.** At what age did you feel this way?

   Note; it is okay to give an age range when the effect started manifesting, just in case you can't remember the exact age. At what age did this first occurred, do you remember the incident that led to it? If yes, narrate it in short words? If not, write only the age and move to the next chapter. Rewrite or add more content when necessary. Especially if you've answered these from the previous exercise.

   _____

   _____

   _____

   _____

2. What happened to your parent at that age? Look beneath the memories they share; identify the deep tragedies they refuse to share; it might be difficult as these traumatic experiences are forever buried in time. What happened to your parent at that age? Describe the event in the boxes below.

   _____

   _____

   _____

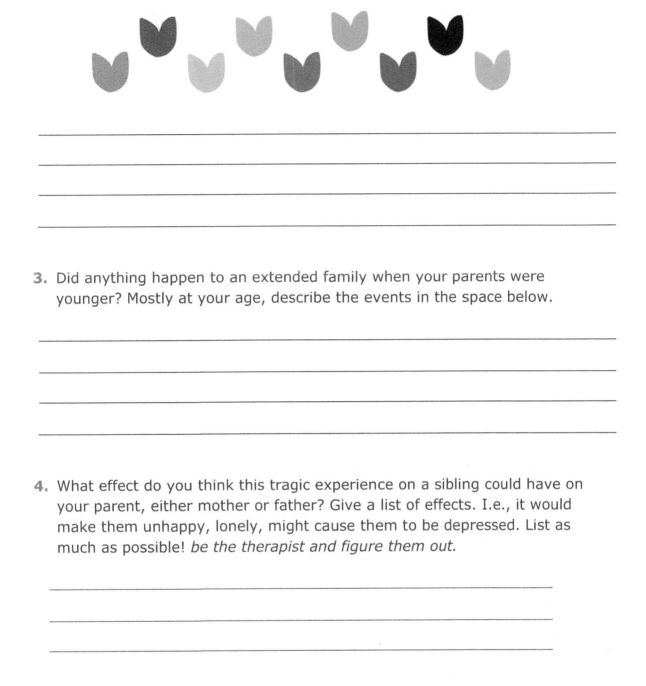

_____

_____

_____

_____

3. Did anything happen to an extended family when your parents were younger? Mostly at your age, describe the events in the space below.

_____

_____

_____

_____

4. What effect do you think this tragic experience on a sibling could have on your parent, either mother or father? Give a list of effects. I.e., it would make them unhappy, lonely, might cause them to be depressed. List as much as possible! *be the therapist and figure them out.*

_____

_____

_____

Visualizing Your parents and their history

Visualizing your parent experience from the stories they shared with you could put you in the best position of embracing and reconnecting with them. It gives you a better understanding of their suffering, pains and trauma. Most

importantly it gives you the opportunity to release these emotions in healthy patterns.

Imagine any of your parent mostly those traumatised. Imagine them standing on the scene of their traumatic experience, visualise them, surrounded by all the horrible situations they might have gone through—using stories they told you.

Take a moment to imagine how difficult it must have been for them to experience and bear with the consequences of these traumas.

Here is a guided pattern for visualizing your parent traumatic history

- Close your eyes and recall all of your parents family's stories and all the catastrophes you've heard about.
- Imagine your mother as a young lady, a small child, or even a small baby, clenching her fists against the waves of grief, attempting to protect herself from the onslaught of her suffering. Relate it with her traumatic experience.
- What does your body feel like as you imagine what she was going through?
- What are the sensations and where in your body do, they occur?
- Can you imagine or feel what she must have gone through?
- Does this strike a chord with you? Do you have any sympathy for her?
- You can go ahead and repeat the process, till you fully reconnect and are able to end the cycle.

Ending the cycle:

Living with inherited trauma can feel like carrying a heavy burden on your shoulders without knowing about it. It is being in chain and not even know. Once you realise you carry this burden or have these chains limiting you, then you can take a bold step and let the burden or chains off your life. For some patients, discovering the origin of the problem is enough to offer a sense of

freedom from the trauma they have carried for so long. You realise the burden you carry isn't yours and the emotions you feel aren't a direct result of anything that might have happened in your life. Rather, the result of an event that took place even before you were born. The realisation is a tremendous leap to recover for some as this reduces the stress on them, enabling them to be more focused on their recovery.

But what might be seen as a tremendous leap to recovery for some patients may just be a step for other patients. In order to attain visible progress, the discovery of the origin of the trauma needs to be accompanied by active exercises and experience that will cause positive change to the body. Most of these exercises and daily routines, practices are in this book.

So how do you end the cycle?

1. **By identifying the traumatic events in your family history;** identifying the traumatic events that occurred in your family could be a first step in overcoming these traumas. By doing these, you identify recurring images, words, or emotions that may be linked to the history of your family. It could also be seen in the behaviors of members of your family. Throughout this section, we've taken time to identify the traumatic events that may have occurred in your family history.

2. **Make peace with your family history;** identifying the origin of these traumas, though the first step isn't enough overcoming inherited traumas, but putting together effective plans and patterns for making peace and letting go of every inherited emotion. Section two of these books are summed up exercise and strategies effective for your healing.

Working Through Genogram

A genogram is a tool common among therapists that are into family therapy. Throughout history, families have passed on pieces of themselves to the next generation. These can be illness, valuable or beautiful objects, such as stories, culture, knowledge, or belongings. This is where Genogram comes in. A family's genogram provides a way to examine these patterns and to clarify those strengths and weaknesses. Genograms provide the groundwork for nurturing generational strengths and eliminating weaknesses. As a therapeutic tool, a genogram can be used to best access the situations and the reaction of the people involved in a traumatic situation. It also helps in devising ways for reconciliation, as well as mending family relationships.

A genogram shows off not only the medical history but also the relationship of the family members across generations. It reveals hereditary loopholes that exist in the relationship between family members. Hereditary and psychological factors which both play a role in the current state of affairs can also be identified through a genogram. Each line and symbol in a genogram represent the emotional connection between each family member.

Genograms play a vital role during the assessment portion of therapy. Not only do they offer insight into your family history, which is a great gain for your recovery, they also inform you of the trauma experienced by any member of the family, and those buried within the family history. Using a timeline along with a genogram helps therapists and patients get a better view on their family history.

Alterations in the way you behave can be caused by problems unknown to even the closest of family members. For example, a child who used to be a bright student in school suddenly became moody, rebellious, and a truant. The child may hesitate from sharing his problem in the presence of a therapist or anyone at all. Therapists should be able to identify the reason behind the change in behavior without forcing the child to talk about it. Genograms say how an issue has escalated and how it continues to affect the family.

A genogram helps you attain a wider view in dealing with your family issues. In putting right family relationships, it's required that each member avoid attacking, defending, or disregarding anyone. Genogram helps you see that the hindrance to a peaceful resolution is the attitude and overreaction. A genogram isn't all about pinpointing the weaknesses in the family relationship. It can also identify strengths that will act as a support towards full recovery from inherited family trauma.

Drawing genograms improves communication in the family, since the process entails some questions that only family members can answer. This helps make the relationship between the members strong as they discover new things about themselves and their bonds with each other.

In this section, we will create our family tree, two generations back. The aim is not really to know their names or residence but to connect their experience by doing your own research.

Your Present Family Generation Tree

In this section, we would use a simple family genealogy to illustrate and identify the inherited traumas in our present families. By identifying the stories that resonate pains or bring back tears, whatever the case may be, take your time to ask your immediate parents for questions, clues and note everything. At the end of this chapter is a family tree and other helpful tools for uncovering the hidden trauma.

There are two major types of family tree. The first is the primary family tree; which comprises your immediate family together without their family linage. It comprises your siblings, parents, grandparents without acknowledging your aunties, uncle or step relatives. Whereas in secondary generational, the chart is extended to contain your parent and their siblings, your grandparent and siblings, as well as your cousins and extended relative.

In extended family tree, the range of family members included is limited to those with resonating inherited emotions or those once affected with trauma.

Steps to setting up your own family tree.

For each family member;

Write out a notable characteristic of each of the family member. What was the most significant character of such persons, how was their life? When you ask others about them how is the reaction of others. Are their events In their life that were traumatic or created scars? Write everything out. Break each character into smaller bits and figure out which one felt the same way or is responsible for your inherited emotions.

The following are important areas you should take note of;

- Their Behaviors when they were younger or even now. How were they on a general note

- Notable events; were they once victims of traumatic events

- How people feel about them; how was people perceptions of them, were they regarded as too anxious, always angry, or where they always affected by mood swings and bipolar disorder. Irrespective of the case write them out.

- Social activities; were they engaged in a social activity, what did they enjoy doing, what gave them happiness, and what made them sad. Also ask about their social friends how they behaved on a general level.

Here is an example;

This is a family history of an ideal character named **John**. John suffered from chronic anxieties. In his search for a solution, he was introduced to the subject of inherited trauma and was asked to trace the origin of his family history. But remember, always start with yourself and move upwards towards the family hierarchy.

Using one of the tools for drawing family tree, his genealogy was like

My immediate family history.

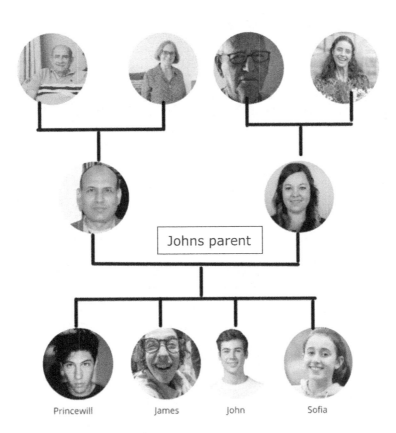

Siblings; PRINCEWILL, JAMES AND SOFIA

Princewill

- **general Behavior;** has anger issue, distorted reasoning, and very strict
- **Notable events;** bullied all through high school. Lost his front teeth during these process
- **How people feel about them;** had very few friends that understood him.
- **Social activities;** had no social activity. Was a loner and enjoyed his own company

James

- **general Behavior;** quiet, low self-esteem, addicted to drugs and alcohol
- **Notable events;** none I can remember
- **How people feel about them;** fun to be with, easily distracted, always afraid and week
- **Social activities;** had no social activity.

john [myself]

- **general Behavior;** depressed, loner, and suffered from social anxiety
- **Notable events;** none
- **How people feel about them;** none
- **Social activities;** none

Sophia

- **general behavior;** SOCIAL, easily irritated, abstract thinking, people pleaser, easily influenced by peers
- **Notable events;** none
- **How people feel about them;** I really don't know.

• **Social activities;** an Instagram model	

Parents [paternal and maternal]

• **general behavior;**
• **Notable events;**
• **How people feel about them;**
• **Social activities;**

He repeated the same for his Grandparents [paternal and maternal] He also linked it to his extended [secondary] family. Including his parents' siblings, grandparents' siblings, etc.

Some online tools to creating your own family tree

- Ancestry.com
- My heritage
- Find my past
- Family tree now
- Crestleaf
- ancestral forest
- Ages online
- Faces tree
- famberry
- family echo
- family mingle
- family pursuit
- family tree online
- Famlu
- let me tree
- our story.com
- the family link
- tribal pages
- Family tree maker
- Roots magic
- Legacy
- Family historian
- Geni.com
- Familysearch.org

Other questions and exercise in realising the inherited trauma

The following question could serve as a guideline for identifying the inherited trauma. Take your time and underline the answers that resonate with your experiences.

1. Is there a topic in your family that family members aren't allowed to talk about, maybe because it's too upsetting for someone? Or it's highly prohibited.

   Yes   None That I Am Aware

2. Has anyone in three generations of your family gone into active combat or sent a family member into active combat.

   Yes   None That I Am Aware

3. Has anyone in three generations of your family experienced a miscarriage or stillborn child.

   Yes   None That I Am Aware

4. Has anyone in three generations of your family immigrated to a new country.

   Yes   None That I Am Aware

5. Has anyone in three generations of your family experienced sexual violence.

   Yes   None That I Am Aware

6. Has anyone in three generations of your family experienced a hate crime, racism, or stigmatization.

   Yes   None That I Am Aware

7. Has anyone in three generations of your family lived through a war fought in their homeland.

   Yes   None That I Am Aware

8. Has anyone in three generations of your family spent a portion of their life in poverty.

   Yes   None That I Am Aware

9. Has anyone in three generations of your family experienced divorce.
          Yes   None That I Am Aware

10. Has anyone in three generations of your family lost a significant piece of their cultural heritage.
          Yes   None That I Am Aware

11. Has anyone in three generations of your family experienced abuse or domestic violence.
          Yes   None That I Am Aware

12. Has anyone in three generations of your family experienced the death of a child.
          Yes   None That I Am Aware

Are there any core precaution resounding in your parenting discipline patterns? Maybe they are fond of telling you to abstain from the opposite sex? Or to avoid men. Whatever it may be, note it.

My mother always frowns, most times yells when she sees male friends among my companies…. TINA said, that was her breakthrough key point.

Do you experience such or do they yell and complain about your lack of staying at home, even when you are often around, in whatever case it is, if it's too severe, then it can be a sign of a traumatic experience.

My mom frequently and obviously taught us to lock the door every single time, adding issue of insecurity, abuse and rape, Lawrence would say.

Most times this could be normal, if done in excesses and attached to it is a compulsive behavior of disruptive emotions then they can indicate an inherited trauma. the effect of these normal events can be identified as a trauma if the history involved a traumatic experience of insecurity, rape or molestation etc. this could also be embedded in your family history. There are many others. Now it's your turn. Are there any resounding instructions or compliance your parents ensure you follow? List them below.

1. _____

2. _____

3. _____

4. _____

5. _____

6. _____

Finally

Regardless of the difficulty of our circumstance, we must each bear it. No one can take on the fate of a parent, grandparent, sibling, uncle, or aunt without experiencing a suffering. You unintentionally carry the feelings, symptoms, behaviours, or challenges of an earlier member of your family system as if they were your own when you are entangled. I believe this chapter has formed the baseline for identifying the inherited trauma and provided you with an insight into ways of overcoming them. In the next chapter, we will look at effective ways to deal with these inherited emotions and experiencing genuine freedom.

EXPOSING THE TRAUMA

CHAPTER ONE

Therapeutic Tools For Continuous Improvement.

As we've seen from previous chapters, most inherited family traumas are experienced differently by various members of the family. And most of these traumas manifest later than post-traumatic disorders, which cause recurrent mental and physical distress to the victim.

From above explanations, various members of the family experience inherited family trauma in different ways and most of these traumas manifest later, causing distress to the victim both mentally and physically.

Generational trauma gives us, as therapists, the lens of wondering; If the present predicament is a pattern of the person's history? And how we can break this cycle? At least get the comfort of understanding and adopting effective ways of dealing with these inherited emotions. In the words of Bessel Van den Kolk, the author of the book "The Body Keeps the Score", the ability to feel safe is "probably the most important aspect of mental health". The aim of this chapter is to enable you to experience "felt safety" which is an empathetic relationship based on the therapist's unconditional acceptance of the individual's thoughts, feelings, and experiences. Doing these would help bring to limelight the "Why do I do this?" behind the negative behavior that is affecting your life.

In these chapters, we would express the different therapeutic tools for overcoming inherited traumas. The exercises here have been simplified into basic comprehensible patterns effective for your recovery.

Healing the traumatised image.

Traumatized images are the ideal experiences of a traumatised victim. They represent the suffering, pain and emotional discomfort the person may have experienced. Whether we're conscious of it, our life is profoundly influenced by a resonating inner image, beliefs, expectations, assumptions, and opinions, most of which are influenced by the inherited genes associated with your family history.

The traumatic image most times may not be visible as they are not traceable or relatable, but an underlying emotion of grief and anxiety usually brings the reminder of an unexplained occurrence from our family history. These underlying emotions show a traumatic image formed in the subconscious mind.

Most traumatic emotions, especially with victims of inherited trauma, are product of an unresolved image of painful experiences, emotions, and hurt that has been suppressed over a long period. When you make the link to what sits behind your unexplained emotions, fears, and anxiety, you are already opening up possibilities for resolution. Sometimes the new understanding is enough to shift the old painful images and start a visceral release, providing you with the satisfaction, peace and control.

To achieve these, we will need sentences, rituals, daily practices, and exercises to help us forge a new inner image. An image opposite to what we currently feel.

For individuals struggling with inherited family trauma, it is needful that they figure not only out the roots of their unexplained emotions but gain a mastery in reforming the image of hurt buried in their subconscious, and embrace a better image of self-reliance, understanding and control. A new image independent of the inherited emotions and experiences. In these sections and others to come, we will focus on reforming your new image. To do these, we would have to adopt practices and other effective tools necessary for your healings.

Rituals for inherited family trauma

Rituals are not necessarily fetish or voodoo like practices, they can be summed up to be obscure habits, patterns, practices or activities that guarantee your freedom from inherited trauma. In this session, we would look at some effective rituals that would aid your recovery from inherited trauma. But note; *if by any chance you feel uncomfortable, please skip this section and move to the next one.*

Some rituals effective for healing inherited family trauma include:

#Ritual one; Placing a photo on the Desk.

Placing a photo on a desk is a ritual adopted and used over a long period, its major aim is to communicate not really with the dead, but as a reference of expressing your emotions, questions and feelings to a person who may not be present or alive.

The aim of this exercise is to comfort and release the inherited emotions back to the owners — The actual victims from your family history.

Before continuing this exercise, you must have known and figured out the parent, uncle, or aunt responsible for the emotions you carry. If not, please go over the first session carefully and more intentionally.

The process involved in actualizing the results of releasing these emotions include.

- Get a photo of the victim of the traumatic experience. — Could be your grandfather, mother or any other" grand siblings" from your family genogram

- Drop the photo on top of a table and sit down in front of it, facing the picture

- Try as much as possible to be calm. You can use any meditating techniques like breathing slowly, counting your breaths, etc.

- Once calm, purposefully create an image through visualisation of the victim of the traumatic event from your family history

- Using your visualization Imagine leaving the guilt feelings with the victims, you do these by repeating the words…. *Take back your feelings. I don't need it. I am a new creature, different and unique. Say these with other healing sentences which are included in this chapter.* Repeat these as much as possible as you meditate.

- You can be more precise by saying the exact emotion you want to let go, "take back your anger", "take back your anxiety", "take back these feelings", "take back this hate", "take back this depression", "take back this anger", "take back . . .", be more precise and repeat it to yourself as much as possible

#Ritual two; Writing A Letter.

Gina lost her mother in a ghastly motor accident few days before she left for the states, still struggled with overwhelming emotions and found it difficult having healthy relationship with others.

She always blamed herself for letting her mom died, she blamed herself for refusing to take her alongside as she was travelling to the states; she blamed and cursed herself every single time.

She came across the rituals of letter writing and it proved to be an effective tool. Although she knew her mom would never receive the letter, she wrote it to her, apologising for her refusal to let carry her along while she was going to the states.

In the letter, she wrote: "I'm so sorry, mom. I know how much you love me and wanted to be with me, and how much hurt my refusal may have caused you. I'm very sorry. I know you'll never be able to receive this letter, but I hope you receive these words." She ended the letter with your beloved

daughter. After writing this letter, she said she felt a sense of peace and security like she had never felt before, one she couldn't explain.

Writing is an effective practice in healing inherited traumas. It involves writing a letter of comfort and release of emotions to the victim, informing him or her of the need to be free from these emotions.

This ritual is called writing a letter of release — releasing the emotions back to them. More on these was broadly expanded and dealt with in the next session.

#Ritual three; Placing a Photo Above the Bed.

This practice is mostly used though not widely accepted, but the practice is common and effective in healing from inherited family trauma. When you hold a picture of a love one that has suffered a traumatic event and reassure the person of comfort. You automatically release the inherited trauma and emotions that has prolonged to you.

Process involved include
- Get a picture of a family member, especially those that were once affected by trauma
- Keep the picture of such person close to you before you sleep
- Look at the image, quietly and mindfully comfort the person
- Imagine the victim as a young child reaching out to you for help, and you giving them the comfort they deserve
- Hug them close and repeat the phrase, "you will be fine", "everything will be alright", "take back your emotions and have your last rest"

#Ritual four; Developing a Supportive Image.

A supportive image is a backup support born from a divine connection or a visual representation of another reference to support, most of which might

be the victim, a holy being, or even an angel. The most appropriate system used where the victims are not known is to imagine an angel from above coming to your aid, taking all your pains and worries and granting you freedom beyond the natural.

Jeremiah had a struggle relating with others. During his therapeutic sessions, he came to the realisation of his inherited emotions and was able to identify the victim responsible for these emotions. But the family member responsible was late and not in view, neither was his picture evidently available. He employed the fourth aspect, which is developing a supportive image, an imagery as reference to the family member he never met or know.

During the process, he visualised a supernatural being, an angel coming to console him, and him sharing the emotions to the angel which will take these messages to the victimised family member,

spencer had issues identifying with others. she always found peace and solitude staying alone, all these happened after her mother died and she was forced to stay with her grandmother. The grandmother, being a traditionalist, had knowledge of these methods of reconnecting with the dead employed this method for her.

During the process, her grandmother had her imagine her deceased mother as a guardian angel protecting them both. She picked out the resemblance between herself and her mom, which was the pointed nose, and reassured her that touching her pointed nose whenever she feels lost would help her in feeling safer and more connected with her mom.

This practice helped her evenly. With time she started opening up and relating to others, her life changed afterwards, knowing that her mom was always looking out for him. she was with her always.

Process for achieving these

- Look for a quiet place, if possible, do these at the pastime of the day in a place free from distractions and movements

- Meditate for few minutes till your body is calm and ready to reconnect with a supernatural being
- Using your imagination, visualise a supernatural being coming to your rescue. Imagine God sending an angel to be with you, to comfort you and to give you the peace and love you need. If possible, say a prayer or two, involve in a worship.
- In other cases, you can imagine your mother, father or any of the victim coming to meet and receive the words you have to say
- Express yourself to them in the best possible way
- And finally imagine them leaving with these emotions, as you wave a farewell to them.

#Ritual five; Creating a Boundary.

Boundaries are one of the most accepted conditions used for treatment of most mental health cases. Boundaries are effective tool for separation, for identification, for differentiation and for realisation. For healing inherited traumas, boundaries entail you return the inherited emotions back to the victims, also creating a wall of protection for these emotions not to resurface again.

Processes involved include

- Set out a time for meditation, mostly at the earlier time of the day. Free from distractions and noise.
- With a marker, chalk or any other sign, draw a line around your standing point.
- Still staying in the enclosed space, repeat these words.
    A. 'This is my space. You are over there and I am over here'.
    B. 'Your feelings are over there with you and my feelings are over here with me'.

C. 'I'll honour my own feelings.
D. 'Whatever you once felt, I return them back to you'.
E. 'Henceforth, I decide to be free from these traumas'.
F. 'I return them to you; I return them all to you'.

Ever since Sylver was young, her mother had been the breadwinner of the family and was strict and compulsive. Yet never satisfied. So Sylver did everything possible to please her. She never enjoyed a mother daughter relationship like the average teen. Instead, she lived her life in fear and was subjected to her mother's will.

As she grew up, she discovered she has lost the power to decide for herself, as she kept relying on the decision of her mother and other persons. Though the mom died a few years after sylver had her second child, it became difficult for her — There was no one to take the role of compelling or telling her what to do. There was no one to play the role of decision making for her. to fill the gap she started depending on others for the role her mother played. This, to an extent, affected her marriage and left her with a broken family.

During therapy, she was introduced to the practice of setting boundaries and separating herself from her offenders. She sat on the floor and traced a circle around her body using a piece of chalk, after drawing the line around to form a complete circle she imagined her mother on the other side of the line, outside of the circle and enforced the boundaries by telling her mother:

"Mummy I have always depended on you for the decision making of my life. I have always done things to make you happy and uphold your decisions, even to my detriment. Now it has complicated everything and I'm left with myself and suffering. Mom, from now on, I decide to let go. You have no say in my life. I won't depend on your counsels and opinions. Henceforth, I take full control of my life and action. I would make and uphold my decisions even if it is detrimental.

Your feelings are over there with you and my feelings are over here with me. Your decisions and opinions are over there while mine are here. In this boundary, I'll honour my own feelings and decisions without having to involve you or other people".

She repeated this process few more times, and meditated while she did it, few weeks later her dependency on other people for decisions reduced, and in no distant time she had improved, she developed the ability to decide and enjoyed the consequences and blessings of every actions.

Creating Personal Healing Sentences

According to the English vocabulary the word healing is the process of recovering or becoming healthy again. So healing sentences are those words spoken that brings about recovery and makes its victim healthy mentally, emotionally and in most cases physically. Healing sentences are phrases which brings a sense of relief to your traumatized body. They are sentences that triggers the healing process especially in the healing of an emotionally disturbed person. Healing sentences are effective tool for overcoming the effect of inherited trauma. They are words spoken to the universe issuing an attraction of positivity. They are words of comfort, symbols of hopes, and brings relief when they are spoken to its victims including ourselves.

Biblical scriptures to aid the healing process

The bible contains the written words of God which can never fail or b broken. Believing and meditating on this word could send a sense of relief to every inherited emotion and feeling. While reading the bible it is necessary that you meditate on it. By meditating you are causing more light to emerge and your understanding brighten. Also declare and believe it would work.

Matthew 11:28 "Come to me, all you who are weary and burdened, and I will give you rest."

Isaiah 40:29 "He gives strength to the weary and increases the power of the weak."

Psalm 147:3 "He heals the broken-hearted and binds up their wounds."

Mark 5:34 "He said to her, 'Daughter, your faith has healed you. Go in peace and be freed from your suffering.'"

Psalm 30:2 "Lord my God, I called to you for help, and you healed me."

Isaiah 41:10 "So do not fear, for I am with you; do not be dismayed, for I am your God. I will strengthen you and help you; I will uphold you with my righteous right hand."

3 John 1:2 "Dear friend, I pray that you may enjoy good health and that all may go well with you, even as your soul is getting along well.

Revelation 21:4 "He will wipe every tear from their eyes. There will be no more death or mourning or crying or pain, for the old order of things has passed away."

Here are some personal healing sentences effective for your healing. Say these few sentences out loud.

1. 'I won't live to replicate this trauma. My life is what I have'.
2. 'I promise to live my life fully'.
3. 'I promise to do something tangible in my life'.
4. 'This trauma has to end with me'.
5. 'I'll honour you for going through all this'.
6. 'I'll light the part of darkness'.
7. 'I'll make something significant out of this catastrophe'.
8. 'Now I understand, you made me understand'.
9. 'I am in charge of my own happiness'.
10. 'I am in control of my life'
11. 'Everything in life happens for me'
12. 'My thoughts and feelings matter'.

13. 'I decide to be free from these inherited emotions'

14. 'Every feeling can be managed'

15. 'I'm separate from my inherited emotions'

16. 'I released every inherited emotion back to the owner'

17. 'Now I know,, I am free'

18. 'I am a successful person'.

19. 'I am confident in everything that I do'.

20. 'I am doing the best I can'.

21. 'I choose to be happy'.

22. 'I am in perfect health'.

23. 'I am resilient; I will get through this difficult time'.

24. 'I believe in myself'.

25. 'I do not have anxiety'

26. 'I choose to remain calm and focus'

27. 'Everything will be fine'

28. 'I am a better version of myself'

29. 'I do not have anger'

30. 'My emotions are not overwhelming but easily controlled'

31. 'I cultivate inner calmness'

32. 'I am free from my inherited emotions'

33. 'I have everything I need'

34. 'I am in control of my emotions, thoughts and feelings'

35. 'The past is now passed'

36. 'I am redeemed to be a better person'

37. 'This is me, the new manager of my life'

38. 'I love me'

39. 'I am valued, loved and separate from my inherited emotions'

40. 'I am strong, needed and important'

Get rid of these negative sentences

Negative sentences are unhealthy coping skills the body unconsciously adopts when threatened, scared, or emotionally unstable. They are sentences said when faced with fear, anxiety, or even anger. Negative sentences are harmful to your inner child. They are threats to your mental health, affect your emotions, belittle your faiths and destroy your esteem. To overcome the inherited trauma, you must shut the voice of these negative emotions. Don't let it voice out negativity, don't let it cripple your esteem and confidence. Don't let it, don't let it. Here are examples of negative sentences that limit your healing process. Are there more you can relate to? write them out in the space below

- I'll be rejected.
- I'm not sufficient.
- I'm too much.
- They will leave me.
- They will hurt me.
- They will betray me.
- I won't exist.
- It is hopeless.
- I won't get healed.
- It is over.

Are there more? Write it in the space below.

_____

_____

_____

_____

_____

_____

_____

Decreasing the effect of your trauma through writing

The effect of trauma can best be reduced by writing, not just in your journals but as a letter addressing it to a particular person, address and date. you can address the letter to the past with a date when the victim was still alive, or even addressing the letter as though the victim still lives and is present with you. Writing about these thoughts and feelings is called 'expressive writing` or `descriptive writing' and it's an effective tool for recovery for most victims of trauma, as well applicable to those suffering from inherited family trauma. Expressive writing places a greater emphasis on the individual's feelings than the occurred events, memories, or people.

Processes involved

- Find a quiet time and place with no distractions. Don't be concerned, however, if there is some noise. Some people find writing at a coffee shop, bus station, on a bus, or even during a five-minute break during the day very helpful. Once you're done writing, reread what you wrote and pay utmost attention to how you feel. Pay attention to any changes in your thoughts or feelings because of the writing you do.

- Write about the same topic for at least three more days. writing about the same topic on successive days can help put you through and as well, improve the clarity of your thoughts about a traumatic event. You will be surprised at the amount of clarity and healing that writing can bring. Spellings or grammar shouldn't be your worry. Focus simply on pouring out your thoughts and feelings relating it with traumatic experiences of your parents or grandparents.

- Try to be as descriptive as possible. For example, when you're describing your feelings, write about the thoughts connected to those feelings and how those emotions felt in your body. This will help increase your consciousness and the clearness of your emotions and thoughts.

- You may find it overly helpful to keep the things you write so that you can look at it to see how your thoughts and feelings have changed while using this therapy process.

Here is an example

Hello mom

I felt terrible being abused by my step dad. I've concealed these feelings for so long now. It has affected my grandchild. I concealed it to protect your happiness and marriage. I never wanted you to feel bad knowing such a horrible thing occurred. I love you, mom but I have to let go for my child's sake. I do not want the emotions to transfer to them. I refuse to transfer these horrible feelings to them. As a result, I am releasing these motions to you in the best possible way I know best.

Your daughter gloria

Here is another from **glory Kelly** to her late uncle.

To my uncle paul Kelly
        Dear uncle

Growing up, I have seen you humiliate and abuse my family as though we were not related to you, especially after the death of my father, ever since I had wished to tell you, but I was too small and feared you would shout at me. My prolonged wish continues till you died in an accident. To be sincere, I was happy when I heard the news, but then I regretted not telling you how I felt before you passed on. Now I'm stuck with these feelings and I over react at every point in time. I am caught in a web of prolonged self-defence and I over react as if the world was you.

Henceforth, I am releasing these emotions back to you. I do not want to see the world like a predator zone. I wouldn't want to overreact at the slightest of all mistakes. I've enjoyed life as it comes.

Your niece Glory k. Kelly

Now it's your turn,

    in the space provided or in your journal, write a brief but direct letter to your parent or the victim of the traumatic experience from your family history.

_____

_____

_____

_____

_____

_____

_____

_____

_____

_____

_____

_____

_____

CHAPTER TWO

Trauma From Family Separation And Toxic Parenting

A home, they say, is a place where members of a family spend time together in peace, harmony, with love and showing support for each other. But my home was the opposite. I never had this definition of home, nor that of a family. I was born into a perverse polygamous family. My dad keeps bringing children into the world with different women, and somehow, they all end up staying under the same roof. My dad, is legally married to 2 wives, my mom being the second wife, and his many night stand encounters. The house was populated with different individuals having the same dad but different mothers, most of whom never stayed with us.

After the baby was born, my mom came in. She was a principled lady and feared what people would say and think of her. This made her force my dad into marrying her as a second wife, even though it was not his decision at first. This complicated her life and somehow, she blamed me for everything.

"Why did you choose to destroy my life?" she would say.

"I was a tall, beautiful girl, who was admired and cherished before you came and spoilt everything," she claimed. She never treated me like her child. She always saw me as a curse to her, a pain to her happiness, a stake in her heart.

In her divorce statement, she claimed that both of us were bad luck for her and that she will regret her actions for the rest of her life. I endured these agonies because it was a reality I had to accept and move on from.

But moving on... Can I really move on?

Growing up, I never understood the meaning of love. My dad had no time. He was never at home, nor was he ever available to hear the complaints of his children. The only thing he did was provide money. Of course, he could because he was a

wealthy business executive affiliating with notable companies, working round the clock, yet having no time for his children.

Fast forward to this day. I never understood what it felt like to be loved. I saw every feeling of love as infatuation or a mirage to either exploit or use for appraisals. I believed none of it. I lived my life playing and toiling with the hearts of many, as well as leaving others broken. To me, freedom, independence, and enjoying life to the fullest were words that came to mind. I did not know that 80 percent of my selfish emotions, beliefs, and thoughts stemmed from my traumatic childhood experiences. Though not inherited, it affected my love life and complicated my entire life. I hated what my parents did, but somehow, I see myself doing the same to my wife and only child. I came across the subject of inherited family trauma, and since then I have been seeing notable differences. At least I can develop these connections with my wife and child. I am seeing my wife as the lovely girl I once proposed to and not as a mistake. *Jake Tomberlin.*

Here is another story from Jidenna.

My parents lived and worked in Nigeria, while I stayed with my elder brother in Inglewood, Los Angeles, United States of America. I stayed with them from the age of four and stayed with them for almost 17 years. During this time, I hardly saw my parents. All I knew was that they were in Nigeria and we were from Nigeria. Though we talked almost every week and she came most of the time to see me, I never had this connection with her. Though she tried her best by calling and sending lots of gifts, I never had that feeling of satisfaction that she was my mother.

I stayed with my elder brother, who was married and had two children, and most of the time I was referred to as his child. His wife was wonderful to me, but most of the time, these feelings of it not being my child still crept in. I felt this void and lacked the emotional care and support my actual parents would have given me. In most cases, I was treated as an outsider, and told several times to go meet my mom. It was a painful experience.

I grew up amidst all these feelings, and unknown to me, these patterns of disconnection had affected my life, thinking patterns, and even emotions. My disconnection with my parents has left a void which has developed into a monster with absurd thinking patterns, behaviour and characters. I was different. I saw the world as a selfish place, and each individual handled themselves alone. This belief prevented me from making genuine friends or creating healthy connections without feeling cheated, exploited, or neglected.

Sooner than later, I became depressed. I lacked friends. Social media wasn't really social to me as it opened the way to more depression. Seeing the way individuals bonded and had fun made me think how neglected I was. My grades dropped; my friends left. I was alone, bored and depressed. My childhood experiences have developed, and he was hunting me.

****

One of life's pervasive and frequently overlooked symptoms is the trauma that results from a dysfunctional family or toxic parenting. Any child that experienced any form of separation from their parent would develop a toxic pattern of thinking and behaving that would reciprocate into the world. Such a child may grow up with anxiety, low self-esteem, or even selfish attitudes and behaviours amid others. A disconnection or interruption between the parent and child would create a void that might develop into a series of complications in the general psychology of the child. A child with this condition usually has a distinct core language that reflects their inability, cravings, and void. In these chapters, we will look at how the childhood experiences of any individual can prolong an experience which could disrupt the general wellbeing of the child for life. Most inherited traumas are because of a disconnection in the mother-child relationship.

Please note that the traumatic experience of your parents might affect the parenting patterns and thus be the reason for their dysfunctionality. When treating such trauma, it is advised that you leave the dysfunctionality aside and address the core issue of their family history.

CHAPTER TWO; TRAUMA FROM FAMILY SEPARATION AND TOXIC PARENTING

Toxic Parenting and Dysfunctional Families.

Parenting is said to be toxic or dysfunctional when parents consistently behave in ways that cause guilt or instill fear in their children. In most cases, this behaviour from the parent may cause the child to act and behave in patterns similar to that of their parent. They may end up resonating the same dysfunctionality as their offspring's. When the bond between the mother and the child is disrupted, because of indifference or dysfunctionality, the stream of negative images can trap the child in a repeated pattern of frustration, self-doubt, fury, numbness, insensitivity to others, etc. This feature is observed largely in sociopathic and psychopathic behaviours.

According to a life lab psychology study in the United Kingdom, the common cause of toxic parents could be traceable to their own childhood history of neglect, abuse, or traumatic experience. For this reason, the topic inherited family trauma dealt extensively on toxic parenting and how they are affected by their childhood family history or post traumatic stress disorder, etc.

Some common signs of toxic parenting include:

- They are self-centered and don't think about the needs and feelings of others, including their child(ren
- They become excessively dramatic and over react at the slightest situation
- Lack boundaries and ignore the boundaries of others
- They are always possessive and controlling
- They are always demanding and demeaning when their expectations are not satisfied
- In most cases, they are rude, aggressive, and abusive

Some notable languages of toxic parents and what they really mean.

1. **Why are you not like this person or that person?** This language, among others, is used to compare their child to others. Most of the time, the comparisons are done with those that seem better than their children, and

doing this is a tragedy for the child. Comparison, irrespective of circumstance, is unhealthy. Other terms for unhealthy comparisons are: why can't you behave, speak, or walk like James? Why can't you be as smart as Jude? and why can't you do like John? In most cases, the comparison is done with siblings.

2. **You are too skinny, fat, or short:** Descriptive condemnation of one body posture, physiology, or defect is a familiar term used by toxic parents. They find a weakness and use it against you. They detect a unique feature about you and use it to criticize, shame, or belittle you. Irrespective of the condition, such an act is toxic to the mental health of the child.

3. **You are a failure. Why did you perform worse in exams?** Most parents unconsciously condemn a child's inability to succeed, which can be normal, but if it becomes a routine or if it happens frequently, then it could be classified as toxic, too. Most parents that relatively condemn their children's actions do it to humiliate them.

4. **I have always told you to keep your mouth shut when you're in public:** most parents that say such things are usually associated with excessive control, which might be a problem. Such acts are characterized by frequent manipulation, bending the child to walk and behave in patterns mandated without giving the child an option to make a choice or discover their own part. Such actions prevent the child from becoming independent in the future. Thus, either making them codependent or easily manipulable by others,

5. **At your age, I was more brilliant and better than you. I wonder what you look like.** Such words are part of unhealthy comparison, which can drive the child into frustration and try to meet the expectations and desires of their parents. Failure to meet expectations can lead to depression. Parents must and should allow their children to develop at their own pace.

Separation

Unlike toxic parenting, where both parents may be present or still together, separation involves two distinct parents not living together, either divorced or physically distant from each other. The effect of family separation on a growing child can create a void of disconnection from separated parents and their offspring. This void may later develop to become a defect in the thinking patterns and general psychology of life. Separation can exist in two forms.

- Emotional separation
- Physical separation

Emotional separation;

Emotional disconnection can result from the inability of a mother to attend to the emotional needs of her children. It can also arise from toxic and dysfunctional parenting, whereby neither the mother nor the father are available to provide the emotional needs of the child, so they stop their focus and attention from being sporadic. The child does not feel secure or safe, even when staying around them, communicating these feelings to them. Every child is entitled to the emotional and energetic presence of their mother as much as their physical presence. The inability of the parents to attend to the emotional needs of the child can be because of the traumatic events and experiences she once encountered.

Below are examples of emotional disconnections because of the emotional trauma of your mother.

Loss of health

If a parent is not physically fit or has any complications in their health, this may affect their interaction with their children as they are always needy, tired, in pain and not healthy. Health complications pose a significant risk to a child's psychology because they cause the child to adopt certain coping mechanisms that may develop into monsters that hunt their life over a long period.

Growing up, Tracy's dad always suffered from diabetes. As a result, she never had the emotional connection with her dad, but saw him as helpless, needy, and demanding. He died when she was fourteen years old. The latter part of Tracy's life was a mixture of guilt, needy.

How *Growing up with a sick parent influences a child.*

- Low self-esteem.
- Communication difficulties.
- Language and cognitive disorder.
- A disruption in their relationship with their children as they never had one.
- Also cause severe pathological consequences, like prolonged grief and unstable emotions.

Loss of pregnancy

Effect of loss of pregnancy to the mother and those around
- Grief
- Anxiety
- Depression
- Struggle to manage the needs of other children

Loss of a parent

In most cases, losing a parent is the most common form of emotional disconnection between a parent and their children. When the parent, either mother or father, is no longer available to provide the emotional needs of the child, it can make the child develop some negative coping measures to tackle their absence. In most cases, they rely on others for emotional support and comfort to replace that which they never receive. Such people end up becoming codependent and having the same effect on their unborn children.

Losing a partner

Losing a partner can send the other partner into a spiral of grief, mourning, and, in most cases, depression, as they see themselves taking on the duties of their lost one, including their debts, struggles, and fears. The remaining partner, faced with these challenges, may find it difficult to connect with their children emotionally or even physically, as they might work round the clock to pay for the mortgage or provide for the family.

Loss of a home

According to habitat.org a Home is a safe haven and a comfort zone for members of a family. It is a comfortable place where physical, emotional, and social support are given to a person. A home is an environment that accepts and treats its members in favorable patterns that make them comfortable.

In most cases, parents that were once thrown out of their homes, because of breakups, financial difficulties, or whatever the case may be, end up struggling for survival. In most cases, they regret their mistakes, and this continuous cycle of regrets could complicate their lives, making them depressed and, in most cases, suicidal.

In this cycle of struggling for survival, accompanied with series of regrets, the parent may lose their connection with the child and cannot provide the emotional needs and support the child really needs.

Physical separation

Unlike emotional separation, physical separation occurs when the parent is physically unavailable to provide for the physical and emotional needs of their child. In most cases, the parents may either be far apart or separated because of divorce, death, or other health complications. This form of separation may develop in the child as a characteristic feeling of loneliness, neglect, and isolation. It gives

the child the impression that they are alone and must take care of themselves at all costs.

Dangers of physical separation of a mother and her children.

- Anxiety
- Post-traumatic disorder
- Depression
- Low self-esteem
- General distrust for others
- Poor social skills
- Socio moral immaturity
- Most times, they may experience regressive behaviors such as bedwetting or irritating characters

Exercises for you

1. Do you feel separated from your parent, your mother?

Yes, I Do   No I Don't

2. If somewhat kind of separation, did you experience? Underline or circle the one. Circle both if both of them relate with your experiences.

Physical Separations   Emotional Separations

3. Why did you choose any/all of them? Give your reasons below.

_____

_____

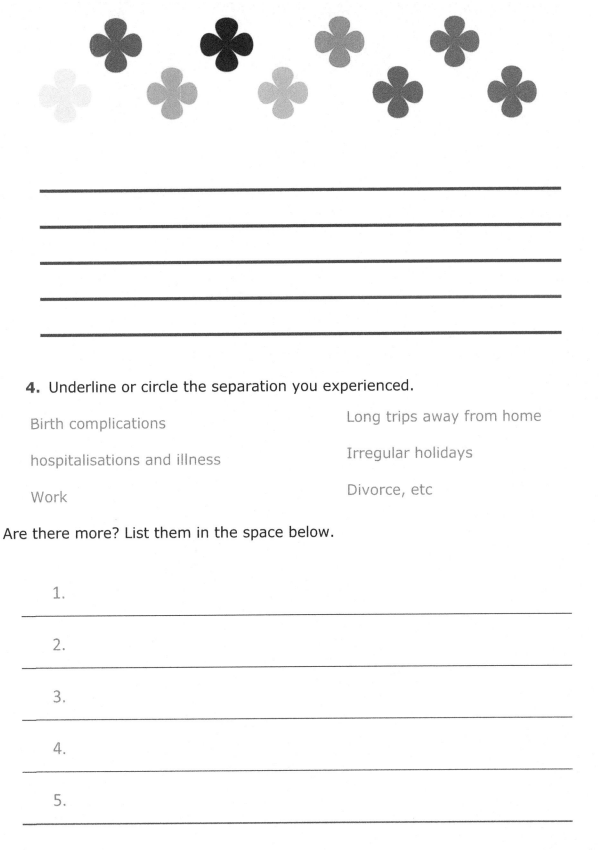

_____

_____

_____

_____

_____

4. Underline or circle the separation you experienced.

Birth complications

hospitalisations and illness

Work

Long trips away from home

Irregular holidays

Divorce, etc

Are there more? List them in the space below.

1. _____

2. _____

3. _____

4. _____

5. _____

Exercises: Were you separated from your parents?

In this section, we will examine the effect of a separated parent on their children. We would use the three core themes to identify the trauma and inherited emotions from our family history.

Using the core sentences from an early separation

Most people that once struggled with family separation usually have some core languages that resonate with their childhood neglect, fears, anxiety, and other emotional instability that may have developed because of the family separation.

Which of the following was the sentence of your early separation? Underline them from the list below.

I'll be left out	They will betray me
I'll be abandoned	I am too much
I don't matter	I am not enough
I'll be helpless	No one wants me
Nobody will be at my house.	I am worthless
They don't want me	They will leave eventually
They will leave me.	I am alone
I won't exist	I am lonely
It's hopeless being with me	I can't let anyone in
I'll be destroyed	No one will let me in to their live

Are there more? Write them down below?

_____

_____

_____

_____

_____

How do you feel saying these?

In this section, we would identify our emotions and how they resonate when our core sentence surfaces. Do you exhibit any of the following whenever you say the sentences listed above? Tick ✅ In Front of any one of them.

Frustrated

Self-doubt

Rage

Numbness

Insensitivity

Anxiety

Worries

Hyperactivity

Fear

Anger

Mistrust

Hostility

Social isolation

Suicidal thoughts and actions

eating disorders

Overwhelming guilt or shame

Exhibiting destructive behaviours

Trouble concentrating

Easily startled or frightened,

Difficulties in expressing positive emotions

Feeling detached

Difficulty in maintaining close relationships

Memory problems

Hopelessness about the future

Negative thoughts
about oneself

Developing trust issues

Memories of abuse

Highly sensitive

Using the tool of core description

In this section, you are expected to describe the separation. The individuals involved, here are some examples.

- Mum is cold. She never held me. I didn't trust her at all.

- My mother is always busy. She never had time for me.

- My Mum and I are really close but she likes my little sister.

- I really don't want to be a burden to my mum.

- My mum and I are not really close.

- I'm closer to my dad than to my mum.

- My mother is so self-centered. It's always about her. She never showed me any love.

- My mother is so manipulative I don't feel safe with her.

- My Mum is not so toxic.

Now it's your turn

1. Which of your parents did you feel a disconnection with?

    My father,   my mother   the both of them

2. What type of disconnection did you feel?

Emotional disconnection,   physical disconnection

3. Describe your mom. Your focus should be on their disconnection, and unavailability, etc.

_____

_____

_____

_____

_____

Some Questions to Ask When Looking for an Interrupted Bond

The following question might be beneficial in unfolding the link of an interrupted bond between your immediate family; most especially your mother and you.

- Did anything happen to your mother while she was pregnant with you? Was she nervous, depressed, or stressed? Describe it.

_____

_____

_____

_____

- Did your parents have any traumatic encounters or problems with each other during or before her pregnancy.

  _____

  _____

  _____

- Were you and your mother separated soon after birth? Did you have a traumatic experience or were you taken away from your mother at an early age? If yes, why did it happen?

  _____

  _____

  _____

- Were you physically separated from any of your parents? If yes, how did you get separated?

  _____

  _____

  _____

  _____

  _____

- Were you physically separated from both parents or just one of them? If yes, who was it? And how did you feel about staying with only one and lacking the other.

_____

_____

_____

- What are your coping skills? How did you cope with not having both or either of your parents by your side? Either healthy or unhealthy coping skills, write them all down in the comment below.

_____

_____

_____

_____

Reconnecting the bond with your parent

- According to Wikipedia, a parent is a caregiver for the offspring of their own species. Every parent handles not only giving birth but taking care of their emotional, physical, and even spiritual needs. At some point, when the parent cannot provide these basic needs for their child, it could cause a disruption in the love and care required to fulfill the child's desires. At that point, the role of caregiver for the child is futile.

- In dysfunctional families or families with toxic characteristics, the relationship between parent and child is often missing. And the child grows up lacking this caregiver responsibility. They grow up with severe mental and emotional health complications.

- Reconnecting with a lost parent re-enables these lost tendencies, creating a link between the expected caregiver's responsibility and the child's present state. Doing this helps release the emotions of neglect, hate, or regret that

may have accumulated over the years, thus giving room for acceptance, satisfaction, and happiness.

- Your relationship with your parents is of great essence, and it's mandatory that you rekindle it. Rekindling it doesn't mean accepting their fault to be yours or encouraging them to be more disciplined and committed to treating you in the best possible way. It involves the release of every emotion (hate, fear, neglect, etc.) that may have accumulated over the years, ensnaring you in a continuous cycle of their dysfunctionality. Decide to rekindle your relationship with your parents.

Below are ways in which you can rekindle your relationships with your parents and caregivers.

- To do this, you need to meet your parents and apologize. When doing this, don't allow your emotions or hatred to interrupt the process. Blindly and calmly ask for their forgiveness, ignore your critics and hatred, and say the "I am sorry" word.

- **Send a gift**; for most people, gifts are the quickest way of saying I'm sorry. A gift sends a message of love and the recipient sees such gestures as a signal of forgiveness. Head to the stores, look for their favorites, wrap them up in style and send them as a message. You might go with the gift or send the gift together with a message of "I am sorry, please forgive me". Doing these would help sharpen.

- **Send a letter;** letters can reconcile with your parents and help in expressing your love for them. They say things you may not say during physical interactions. They can also send messages to a deceased parent or divorced parent. To do this, write a letter of apology expressing yourself in the best possible way, put in their address and send it via mail, electronically or physically. Most of the time, it's best to send a physical letter to them instead of the conventional inbox. Where the parents are far apart or late, you can write to their formal address with their name and throw it in a river,

or flip it through the window of a moving car, or any place that you won't have memories of. Doing so releases these emotions and rekindles your relationship with them.

Advantage of rekindling your bond with a parent.

- It brings back the natural role of caregiver, providing you with the benefits that follow.
- It enhances your mood and emotional health.
- It enables you to live independently of emotions, keeping you in charge of your emotions.
- It provides you with happiness, satisfaction, and peace of mind.
- It gives you the opportunity to grow both emotionally, mentally, and otherwise.

CHAPTER THREE

Inherited Family Trauma And Relationships

A philosopher once said that "a human being is a social animal." And true to that, we would discover that as we journey through life, there is always a need. Relationships are needed for growth from birth to death. We all need one another to survive life's sojourn. A baby needs a relationship with the immediate family, especially the mother, from birth. A husband needs his wife and vice versa. As used in this context, relationships encompass blood ties, romantic or marital relationships, workplace relationships, societal or social relationships, and many other types of relationships. All forms of human relationships. I agree we need each other to fulfill our life's purpose. However, sometimes we experience strained or broken relationships. An unhealthy relationship affects the emotions and effectiveness of those involved. In trying to identify some causes of unhealthy relationships, psychologists believe that inherited family trauma has a role in influencing healthy relationships. It has a role in how humans relate to and handle connections. Most people grow up experiencing some trauma that wasn't of their own making but was inherited. These experiences serve as a significant determinant of how warm or cold they act in every relationship. This chapter will discuss inherited family trauma and relationships, with an emphasis on its effects and ways to resolve them. First, however, let's look at some instances where inherited family trauma affects the relationships of those suffering from inherited trauma.

Instances of inherited family trauma and relationships

Below are various instances of inherited family trauma and how they affect various areas of your life.

Workplace relationship:

Andre was experiencing low self-esteem, and this had affected his ability to relate with his colleagues effectively. Everyone around him thought he was a dummy or anti-social. Frequently, he would attempt to break free, but to no avail. He would say to himself, "I am not a dull person," but could not fathom why he behaved. A colleague invited him for lunch and termed it the most boring lunch ever because Andre couldn't sustain a conversation. Heaven smiled at Andre when he consulted a therapist. It was discovered that his grandfather experienced a similar condition and had attempted suicide frequently because he thought the problem he experienced could never be resolved. Therefore, Andre suffered from low self-esteem passed on to him by his granddad. These inherited emotions have prevented him from having a mutual relationship with his co-workers.

Marital Relationship:

Caroline is a beautiful young lady who has come of age to marry but experiences disappointment every single time. The last straw that broke the camel's back was her breakup with Jonathan, who seemed very loving. Jonathan works late into the night and sometimes does not visit her for weeks, though he always calls and texts. During his absence, he would always call, explaining his reasons, but Caroline was displeased. Whenever there was a need to be absent, she would feel rejected, and this posed a great strain on their relationship. He had tried his best to put things in place but couldn't work out till their eventual breakup. Finally, she met a psychologist who helped her to trace it to inherited family trauma. Her mother had experienced rejection as a child, and it welled until her marriage. She frequently fought with her husband over coming home late, which led to their divorce. The same fate kept recurring in Caroline's life.

Other instances of trauma that resonate and affect relationships

1. Aggressive and violent emotions

Fortune was identified as a bully at school. He quickly took offense at people's actions and occasionally went on suspension. He was suffering from fear, anger,

and anxiety, but couldn't help himself. It was later discovered that his grandfather had anger issues, was aggressive and aimed to bully everybody, including his mum. Although Fortune had not yet been born, he, however, had inherited that trait from his granddad. The fear of being looked down on, the belief that superiority is a function of one's strength and ability to intimidate others, was still resonating in the life of Fortune. Most people are affected by the same characteristics; their emotions are clouded most of the time, and their responses are aggressive, if not violent. Such people believe that the best response when provoked is violence and taking offense at the slightest mistake.

2. *Lack of trust*

Angela couldn't trust anybody, even if the person had good intentions. She always saw the world as an exploit zone and the need to always be on the lookout for herself and herself alone. She never trusted her friends, parents, not even siblings that grew up and shared the same bond with her. She became selfish, and this affected her relationship with others. It became so severe that she lost trusted friends. During therapy, she discovered that her lack of trust was an inherited emotion from her grandmother, who was once betrayed by her closest friend and left crippled in the hands of her abusers. In her life, the guilt and hate of being betrayed were present.

The following instances are how inherited trauma can affect the day to day functioning of its victim, preventing the affected person from enjoying healthy relationships or socializing with people. The list goes on and on. Can you relate to any of the stories above? If yes, then this chapter is for you.

How Does Inherited Family Trauma Affect Healthy relationships?

The first harm Inherited Family Trauma does is to influence how you see and treat yourself before it then spills from you to those around you. Remember, *"you cannot give what you don't have".* So, the trauma works on your subconscious mind to

make you believe what you are not. It makes you believe you cannot be better than you are right now. It is from the content of your mind that you then dish out to those around. From that point, your relationships with people experience a break and the interactions deteriorate.

Another way inherited family trauma affects relationships is by breaking down the lines of communication. Like Andre in our first instance, he was having a challenge of communicating with his colleagues, which affected his self-esteem. There are some who, because of the trauma, cannot communicate their needs with their family, loved ones, or spouses. They get offended by everyone's actions, but the fear of rejection and criticism makes them not communicate with anyone, and most times, they take solace in a secluded lifestyle.

Inherited family trauma also has a negative effect on one's effectiveness at work or school. When the relationship with colleagues or classmates is not cordial, it reduces the productivity level. As communication of ideas and information is a vital force for most businesses and schools, most times you discover that there will be times when you do not even want to go to work anymore. With children in schools, they would often make complaints to parents about not going back to school. *"Nobody wants to stay in a place where they are not celebrated."* And because of this, their effectiveness at work or in academic performance drops drastically. Most likely, this will lead to a dropout or getting a sack.

Inherited trauma breaks the bonds of most healthy relationships because of the emotional breakdown it gives to its victims. This leads to unhappy intimacy that is most likely to dovetail into a breakup or divorce. Children who are experiencing this feel unloved and rejected by their parents. Some go into the street in search of love and affection. Husbands or wives may resolve to take solace in extramarital affairs, and this destroys the family bond.

The next big question, which is popularly asked, is how people in relationships respond to inherited family trauma, and how to best minimize the effect and enjoy a happy, healthy relationship.

Some unhealthy ways people Respond To Inherited Trauma in Relationships

- Withdrawal: most inherited traumas are difficult to explain. You don't just know the cause of your mood swings, or your low self-esteem, or the harsh words. In most cases, victims of inherited trauma withdraw from their relationships and from society. They take solace in their own company or at least figure out the problem, most of which might remain hidden all the rest of their lives if the subject of inherited family trauma is not in view.

- Violence: Most people become angry and resolve to use violence when the cause of their emotions is unexplainable. They blame people and things for the misfortune of their life and become aggressive and violent towards those around them. Some become violent towards their family, spouses, friends, colleagues, etc.

- Ill-health/Insomnia: insomnia is a condition where a person loses his memory. Inherited trauma, if left untreated, can cloud a person's mental capacity and ability to reason, which leads to a decrease in the neural functioning of the brain and the body loses its ability to focus and learn, thus resulting in a loss of memory, insomnia, and ill health. Other health conditions associated with inherited traumas include high blood pressure, stroke, diabetes, etc.

- Addiction to drugs, alcohol, gambling, sex, and other forms of pleasure for self-gratification and temporal fulfilment.

How To Reawaken Broken Relationships Resulting From Inherited Family Trauma?

Here, we are going to be looking at a few practical steps together, and I believe these would go a long way in helping you restore that relationship.

- **Trace how it all started.** *Knowing the history of an event or problem is paramount to getting it solved.* Caroline, in one of our instances, was tired of the continual breakups in relationships. She hated herself for always being the problem. She only found a solution to her problem when the therapist asked her to go talk to her mother or inquire about why the problem

persisted. The origin of every situation is very important. Her mum, amidst tears, made her understand the dilemma and how it led to divorce. It was after that narrative that Caroline took the bold step to heal. Can you, like Caroline, trace the origin of that problem?

- **Fix yourself.** Now that you know your problem, the next step is to heal from it. You have identified the inherited trauma; now heal. Take care of the guilt, anxiety, and anger. Take care of the depressed emotions. Heal from all of them. A course, visit a therapist, pick up a workbook such as this, and embrace the steps and procedures for your healing.

- **Learn to love yourself.** More intentionally, remember that the first thing these inherited emotions do is influence how you see yourself. It forces you to look at yourself through the eyes of a victim from your family history. A girl who has inherited emotions from abuse may see the world as dysfunctional and herself as unworthy; a young child whose grandparent siblings drowned when they were young may develop phobias of rivers, oceans, or anything water. A child who inherited emotions from a grandparent who was a slave trade victim may find it difficult to trust strangers, and so on. Even a child whose parents were Holocaust survivors may find it difficult to trade on the stock exchange or engage in any form of investment. Learning to love yourself means rewriting these wrong self-images and embracing an ideal image necessary for your growth and development, an image necessary for your peace and happiness.

- **As you aim to build better relationships with those affected**, it is important that you build healthy relationships with those offended and with future friends. Making peace with a broken relationship is a giant stride towards healing. You might not get the relationship back, but there is a peace that comes with knowing that you are at peace with everyone. This will help you come to terms with your reality. Some individuals grow up with hatred for their parents because of neglect, which is not totally their fault. Because of this, they have made up their minds not to identify with them, which has affected their lives. A disconnection from your family would create an imbalance in your emotions and reasoning. Going back to reconcile those

relationships will aid your healing and relationships with others. Share wonderful memories with them. Talk about the hurt together, let them know you love them and it was not intentional.

- **Express love to those from whom you expect love;** In life, everyone wants to be loved and cared for. In the quest to seek love from others, so many people forget to first love others. You hear people saying "no one loves me". I sometimes asked them, "How many people have you loved the same way you expect to be loved?". The answer is always none or very few. So, when you want to heal from trauma, intentionally work on loving the surrounding people, and they will give you love in return. This enables you to live a happier and more fulfilling life.

- **Do the things that you both love doing together.** This is after you must have talked through the situation. And this happens in a relationship that has been fixed. If the relationship hasn't been defined or maybe the relationship has been harmed, you can do these things with a casual friend, love one, etc. Do you love taking photos together, seeing movies, eating out, traveling, yoga, etc.? Just anything you both did together initially that gave you joy. Do them and you will discover, with time, your relationship will be reawakened and life beautiful again.

Practical Exercises

Take these exercises to help you through Inherited Family Trauma and relationships.

1. Can you relate to any of the instances above? If yes, write about your experience below.

_____

_____

_____

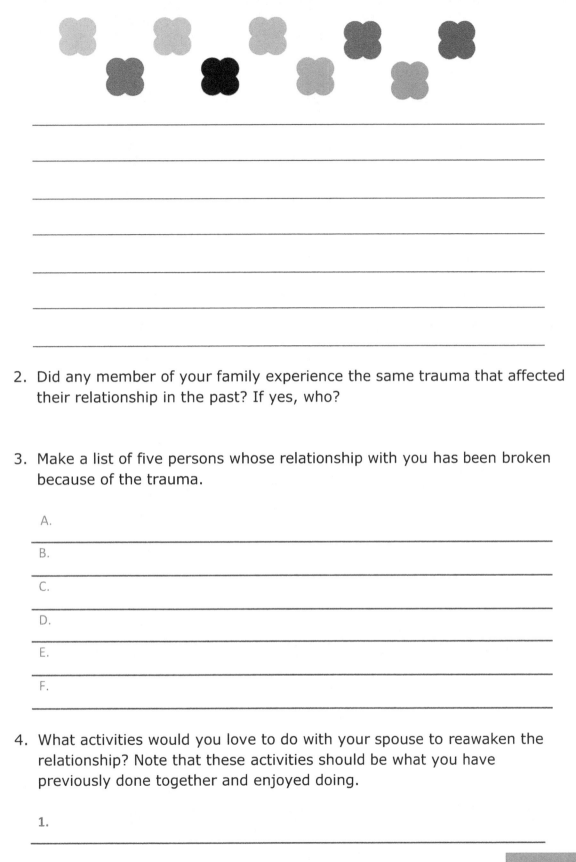

_____

_____

_____

_____

_____

_____

_____

_____

2. Did any member of your family experience the same trauma that affected their relationship in the past? If yes, who?

3. Make a list of five persons whose relationship with you has been broken because of the trauma.

A.
_____

B.
_____

C.
_____

D.
_____

E.
_____

F.
_____

4. What activities would you love to do with your spouse to reawaken the relationship? Note that these activities should be what you have previously done together and enjoyed doing.

1.
_____

2. _____

3. _____

4. _____

5. _____

6. _____

Are there more? Write it in the box below.

CHAPTER FOUR

Inherited Family Trauma And Success

Most people struggle to be successful, no matter how hard they try. It is like a force is limiting their progress and preventing them from making the best of their resources and achieving a result in commendable patterns. Most would say they have a laziness problem or lack the proper organization or structure to achieve their desired results. Beyond the physical struggles, there are underlying beliefs, thought patterns, and emotions that limit an individual's physical results to a large extent. According to a clinical therapist whose primary focus is on cognitive-behavioural therapy, he describes them as a sequence in a series of processes that envelope and impede the result an individual may get. These thoughts and beliefs affect the actions and disrupt the results. The cycle follows these:

An individual who suffers from inherited trauma may find it difficult to succeed because underlying his daily routine lies a struggle of pain, overwhelming emotions, strange reactions, and unexplainable behaviour.

Jane worked with TRANSCORP Hilton hotels for 14 years, but she finds it difficult to get promotions deserving of her experiences and supposed expertise. Most times, when she applied for promotion, her applications were usually turned down based on her inability to handle the demands of the office she desired. Yet they didn't explain why and what she must do to overcome or at least manage the needs of the supposed position. She tried her best to no avail, till she took the bold step to seek help outside her company. During her tour for the right solution, she came across inherited trauma during a live video shared on a group chat on Facebook. She jumped and followed it up, till she could book an appointment.

During the therapeutic session, we could root out the inherited emotions from experiences of her family history. Her grandmother was cheated. She was robbed

of the company she built for 39 years and was left with nothing. In her struggle to get back what belonged to her, she sold off almost everything she had while she kept visiting different courts and lawyers across the state. She lost the case and was devastated. Out of her frustration, she developed a stroke and died not long after.

Jane had the same experiences and emotions running through her DNA, and she had this fear of being robbed of top positions on owning her own company. She always felt used and robbed off. She neither contributed nor put her best effort into her place of work. To a great extent, these limited her chances of gaining promotions. During the therapeutic session, we identified some core languages and struggles, through which I walked her through a series of exercises that enabled her to overcome these traumatic emotions and take complete control of her life. Afterward, her life changed, she became more committed, and a few months later, she was promoted.

Some traumatic experiences associated with failure

To most people, these inherited traumas may manifest in other ways, which may not only limit your promotion but may also improve your general life, time management, productivity, and general effectiveness.

Below are some traumatic experiences associated with the failures of an individual and how they manifest afterward.

1. Low self-esteem and abuse

Jerry Anderson was born into a prosperous family, but struggled with a deficiency. They could not make the right decisions or take risks because they had an inferiority complex and continually could not do things on their own. They relied on their parents for almost everything, which became a major source of concern for the parents. In their search for the hidden cause of their child's inabilities, they came across the term "inherited traumas," from which the hidden cause was found.

Jerry's grandmother, on his maternal side, wasn't born into a wealthy family. She was born into an impoverished family and struggled to make a living, or at least eat. In the process of her struggle for survival, she was raped, and she bore her first child. She became a complete beggar because of shame and work. In most cases, she was subjected to a series of abuses, both physical and sexual. She lost her esteem. When she saw her friend passing, she hid her face; her story was a laughingstock, and she was mocked her entire life. As she aged, she learned a skill from which she could train her children and settle down. But the experience of her childhood, the hindrances, and rape all contributed to her codependency and low self-esteem. And somehow, these emotions were visible in the life of Jerry Anderson, her grandson. Through therapy, we overcame these inherited emotions, and Jerry Anderson could take complete control of his life, emotions, and decisions.

2. Wars

Victims of wars usually suffer from emotional traumas like post-traumatic stress disorder (PTSD), anxiety, and depression or physical traumas like the death of a loved one, severe injury, sexual violence, malnutrition, illness, and other disability, whereas their offspring in the next filial generation may struggle with the same emotions, though not to a great extent. They suffer from inherited emotions like loneliness, low self-esteem, suicidal thoughts, lack of trust, being aggressive, distorted thinking patterns and, in most cases, they cannot work with others.

Inherited emotions from a lineage that suffered from war are usually visible in patterns that may limit their ability to cooperate with others or achieve their desired results.

3. Holocaust survivors

The Holocaust was a period in history at the time of World War Two, which occurred from 1939 to 1945, when millions of Jews were murdered because of who they were, not only Jews but Roma, Sinti, also known as Gypsies, disabled

people, gay people, black people, and even Jehovah's Witnesses. During this time, the Nazis, with Adolph Hitler's help, could take control of major parts of Germany and Europe and persecuted people that weren't considered worthy to be members of society or even worthy of living. During this period, the victims were threatened with a high level of discrimination, maltreated, subjected to forced labour, and even killed in mass. During this process, millions of people were killed, and the rest were forced into idolising Adolph Hitler and upholding the laws and glory of the Nazis.

Most survivors of the holocaust disaster, having gone through their struggles and experiences, unconsciously transmit these overwhelming emotions to their unborn generations. However, its depth and level of overwhelmingness diminishes over time they are. Very visible in their offspring and filial generations.

Victims of inherited emotions from the family histories of Holocaust survivors usually struggle with a part that may disrupt their level of success and expected results. Each victim must take the bold step of ensuring the release of these emotions and taking control of their life.

4. The slave trade and other human rights abuses

Victims of the slave trade are usually bandaged, trafficked from their parent country to a distant land, from which they are subjected to a series of work, pain, hunger, and excessive labour. After that, they may be released or killed. Inherited traumas and emotions from a family history once afflicted with the slave trade usually carry bondage of agony, overwhelming emotions, distorted thoughts, depression, intrusive thoughts, etc. If these emotions are not released and returned, the individual may find it difficult to achieve the level of success they desire.

Do you think you are a failure? Describe why you believe you are a failure. Write about the various encounters that led you to that conclusion.

_____

_____

_____

_____

_____

_____

_____

_____

_____

HOW TO OVERCOME THIS TRAUMA AND BECOME SUCCESSFUL.

Overcoming inherited trauma from family history with cases of wars, abuses, and other kinds of traumatic events and failures requires a level of exercise and detailed inquiries to overcome them. In <u>Chapter Six</u>, there are some practical tools for overcoming these traumas.

Before that, we will look at some crucial factors and helpful tips to consider in order to overcome the effect of inherited trauma on an individual.

Using core identifiers for overcoming these traumas

Identifiers are notable signals or points of reference from which inherited traumas can be traced and identified. It is required in determining the identifier for locating the inherited traumas that are holding you back and preventing you from succeeding and becoming the best version of yourself.

Some identifiers include

- Using the Core Language

- Observing the distorted and interrupted emotions

- Considering the Basic Patterns of Reasoning and Thoughts, etc.

Using the core language approach

From previous chapters, we've seen the importance of the core language in retracing the source of inherited trauma and understanding the dynamics beyond inherited emotions. In this section, we will use core language to identify and neutralize the effect on our bodies as it affects our success.

Your core languages are the repeated words, a language that is embodied in the subconscious but is repeated during stressful events or when they are triggered. For example, what is your core language when faced with failure? How do you respond to a failed goal, an unrealized opportunity, or unsuccessful attempts? What are your stress languages at these points? They could be good indicators from which you can address the inherited emotions and unravel the traumatic experience which may have been ignored, buried, or hidden amongst the family history.

In the aim below, we will use the core language to identify and neutralize the inherited trauma.

1. Have you experienced any level of failure in the past, such as failed marriages and relationships, failed exams, failed job interviews, or other cases where you merited an opportunity but were denied it? If so, list them in the space below.

Take an example... I have experienced a failed marriage. I could not get admitted into the university of my choice, etc.

1. _____

2. _____

3. _____

4. _____

5. _____

Are there more? write them in the space below?

1. Describe the event that happened,

_____

_____

_____

_____

_____

_____

2. Identify your core language.

What do you complain about when any of the events listed above happen to you? Note it is very possible you may not be in the best position to remember. In such cases, you must get a friend or your family friend, or partner to help you identify it. For more information and advanced techniques, refer to the last chapter of this book.

_____

_____

_____

_____

_____

_____

Observing the Distorted And Interrupted Emotions.

To some people, failure is always an awful experience at first, but easily overcome with time. In contrast, to the rest, a single failure in their early life could trigger an inbound on their emotions, thus preventing them from making further attempts to be successful, or even overcoming the trauma of their onetime failure, or even living their life to the fullest. Your emotions may be an indicator of inherited traumas or emotions and how they affect your level of success.

In this section, we will observe these distortion emotions as it relates to one's family history. The aim of these exercises is to examine if the effects of family history would affect the basic patterns of thinking and general emotions as they affect one's success and accomplishment in life.

Observing an interrupted emotion.

 To observe a distortion in one's pattern of thinking and emotions, refer to Chapter Six of this book, which includes a list of some therapeutic tools that are adequate for your recovery.

Considering the Basic Patterns of Reasoning and Thoughts

Have you ever met a person with a thinking pattern that's different from others or entirely weird? Seraphine had a distortion in her thinking pattern. She always had an intrusive thought of being gang-raped and molested by the male gender. To a significant degree, this affected the way she interacted with people in the office and at home. During therapy, she was referred to some OCD worksheets, alongside some therapeutic guidelines on inherited family therapy. She could realize the root cause of her problem. This helped her to overcome these thoughts and take complete control of her emotions, fears, likes, and dislikes. Soon, she was completely freed from these thoughts.

Your pattern of reasoning and thoughts can serve as a pointer to show if your success level is being affected. For example, how do you think on an average level outside your comfort zone? Do you always feel frightened, intimidated, depressed, or lonely? Whatever the feeling, it could be a pointer to an inherited trauma. Or perhaps you keep struggling with an intrusive thought, a thought beyond normal. It could be an obsessive thought, or most times, a frightening one.

Below are a few thoughts that may have similarities to an individual struggling with intrusive thoughts.

- Depressive thought of being left behind
- Thoughts of being abused, neglected or intimidated
- Thought of being used and exploited
- Thoughts of being sexually molested
- Thoughts of dying
- Thoughts of not being enough, not completing the task, being lazy, procrastinator, etc.

Now it's your turn.

Are there thoughts you see yourself struggling with? Write them down in the spaces below.

_____

_____

_____

_____

_____

_____

_____

Describe this thought and how it has affected you.

_____

_____

_____

_____

The Impact of Family Dynamics on the success of an individual

Some inherited family trauma affects and limits the success of its victims.

1. Rejecting a Parent Can Impede Our Success.

Rejecting either our parents or guardians can limit our opportunities to become successful. Regardless of the tale we tell about them, how good or horrible they were, or how upset we are by what they did or didn't do, rejecting them has tragic effects on our general response to life. To so many, our connection with our parents is a metaphor for life. If you believe you have got a lot from your parents, inadvertently or not, you feel that you have got a lot from life. And the feeling that we only got a little from our parents might translate to feeling like we only get a little from life. And these can resonate with the feelings of guilt, depression, holistic thinking patterns, and a biased hatred for humanity.

The mother's role is vital in ensuring each child enjoys security, safety, nourishment, and care. A child who does not enjoy or have a taste of these because of their mother's dysfunctionality or absence may be subjected to feeling

isolated, depressed, and unable. Such people may inadvertently isolate themselves from the luxuries of life. It can feel like we never have enough, no matter how much we have.

Rejecting a father could be just as bad as leaving a mother. The role of the father in every family is to ensure stability, security, and the preservation of both family history and family peace. The father is a figurehead for corrections, reproof, and great affection for his family. Even if the father continues to play his role, a person who rejects his father may not enjoy these things. Such a person may feel afraid and unable to handle difficult situations. In the company of other guys, such people may feel uncomfortable or self-conscious. He may even be scared or unable to accept the obligations of being a parent.

2. **We Can Repeat Our Rejected Parent's Life Experience**

Most of the time, we do the things we hate the most about our family. When we reject a parent, a strange symmetry linking us can occur; we can unwittingly walk in their shoes. What we judge as unacceptable or intolerable in our parents' lives can reappear in our life. It can feel like an unwelcome inheritance. For most people and most books, it is assumed that distancing yourself from a family can have a positive impact on your mental health. However, the more you distance yourself from your parents, the less likely you will live similar lives and repeat their challenges. You become and behave more like them. This doesn't mean you should stick with a dysfunctional parent, as this can also affect your perspective on life, but you can cut off from their dysfunctionality without being overwhelmed by it. The solution is in our thinking. You must train yourselves and your minds to overcome these similar patterns of regret and hatred and create a connection that accepts their love and support, even when it seems missing.

3. **An Unconscious Loyalty to Failure**

We don't need to reject our parents to repeat their misfortunes. Sometimes we share an unconscious bond that keeps us mired in a similar experience. Despite our best efforts, we may find ourselves unable to accomplish more in our lives

than they did in theirs. This is true for the Robinson family. He struggled to gain a bachelor's degree after many attempts. His struggle wasn't that he was not intelligent, but he got overwhelmed by the stress of reading, cramming, and understanding subjects entirely different from real-life logic and reasoning. While considering the case, it was discovered that his father had difficulty getting admission during his time, maybe because the chances of gaining admission during his time were difficult, so he opted for trade and became successful. But was trivialized during the industrial revolution, where he lost his touch. The essence of his profession was diminishing and was being swapped with knowledge and information. This developed regret in his father, who at an older age thought it was unwise to go back and gain the skills needed to continue. Somehow, Robinson jr., having been entangled in an unconscious loyalty, continued in his father's footsteps, sabotaging his chances of becoming successful.

Guilt from family history Can Suppress Success

1. Guilts from a family history of exploitation, cheating, manipulation, or harming others may reverberate in the lives of their children. Guilt, like other emotions, can become ingrained in the DNA and be passed down through generations. These inherited emotions of guilt can affect your financial success. Whether you feel guilty, whether you consider the consequences of your actions, you and your children can live meager lives to atone for the guilt or to compensate for the suffering you have caused others.

2. A family who exploited or used the sweat of others without acknowledging or paying them what was due may find the pain and suffering of being exploited resonating in the family lineage. In a book written by **Mark Wołyń,** he gave a story about Ben, who had the core language of "I can't seem to get beyond the level of just surviving." After a series of attempts to get his law practice into the black had failed, during therapy, he recalled his family history.

3. Ben's grandfather was the proud owner and operator of a thriving citrus grove in central Florida. The family's fortune was built on the sweat and toil

of migrant workers, who were paid pitiful wages and barely scraped by. The family of Ben's grandfather was wealthy. Ben was left with nothing at the end of his life. Ben had fallen behind on payments he couldn't pay and loans he owed the bank since passing the bar, and things had only got worse for him. Through treatment, Ben could connect his current position to his family's past. The disadvantage they suffered was directly proportional to the benefit gained by Ben's family. Ben had been re-enacting the workers' anguish, unconsciously linked with them. It was as if by living in poverty, Ben might somehow pay off his grandfather's debt, which he didn't even own.

Conclusions

Your success and failure are affected by your choices, and since your preferences are born out of emotions, inherited traumas influence your emotions to a large extent. From this chapter, we've seen how inherited trauma can determine the rate at which an individual can become successful.

CHAPTER FIVE

Advanced Tools For Overcoming Inherited Emotions

The previous chapter examined some practical therapeutic tools for recovery and healing from inherited trauma. In this chapter, we will take it a little further by introducing some DBT, ACT, and CBT tools to ensure your recovery. Alongside some worksheets and practical exercises effective for your recovery,

Please note that the exercises in this section are not something you can rush, so we employ you to work along with a journal and, in most cases, a therapist.

Some of the therapeutic tools and techniques listed in these chapters include:

- Child-parent relationship therapy (CPRT)
- Cognitive processing therapy
- Dialectical behaviour therapy (DBT)

But first, we must identify the methods that would be most effective for your recovery. In the section below, we will guide you through choosing the proper methods. If any of the previous traumatic experiences resonate with you, mark them appropriately. After that, you can go to the page attached and start the listed exercises.

Are you choosing the proper techniques for your recovery?

In this section, we will walk through the different possible traumatic experiences encountered by most of our patients during consultancy. If anyone resonates or describes the experiences you encounter, answer the exercises that follow. Mark ✔ for yes or no.

My inherited traumatic experiences	Do you experience such?	if You Answered Yes, Consider These Exercises, if not move to the next
I struggle with thoughts of guilt and self-blame.	No _____ Yes _____	CBT techniques: worksheet 11 ACT techniques: worksheet exercises 4 and 5
I have thoughts that upset me. What if they don't like me? What If the worst happens to me?	No _____ Yes _____	CBT techniques: worksheets 3, 9 ACT and DBT techniques: worksheets 4, 5
I have difficulty concentrating.	No _____ Yes _____	CBT techniques: worksheets exercise 1 and 2 ACT and DBT techniques: worksheets 4, 5
I have difficulty connecting with other people.	No _____ Yes _____	CBT techniques: worksheet 31 ACT and DBT techniques: worksheets 6, 10, and 12
I have difficulty identifying my emotions.	No _____ Yes _____	CT and DBT techniques: worksheets 7, 8
I sometimes put myself down, and I'm very hard on myself.	No _____ Yes _____	CBT techniques: worksheet 10 ACT and DBT techniques: worksheets 4, 5, and 11
I feel nervous, anxious, or tense most of the time.	No _____ Yes _____	CBT techniques: worksheets 1 through 2 DBT and ACT techniques: worksheets 5

I have thoughts of hurting myself or attempting suicide	No _____ Yes _____	DBT techniques: worksheet 9, which should be completed with the help of a trained mental health professional

Child-Parent Relationship Therapy (CPRT)

Its principal premise is that parents can provide significant and lasting therapeutic gains in place of a therapist. In child-parent therapy, the parent is the therapy, and they handle their child's traumatic or emotional needs. A supportive group or an environment teaches parents how to respond quickly and effectively to their children's psychological and behavioural needs. Children also learn that they can depend on their parents for acceptance, love, and protection. This therapy enriches the relationship between parents and their children and teaches them to see their child's underlying needs instead of just responding to symptoms. It is especially effective for parents who have witnessed a traumatic event and would not like their child to inherit these emotions. More on this subject will be broadened and expanded in our subsequent book. Please stay tuned or check your bookstore to update its release.

Few exercises you can do as a parent in dealing with your child's inherited emotions

1. Identify noticeable symptoms in your child. One of the few exercises you can do as a parent in determining if your child is suffering from inherited trauma is by tracing out notable symptoms in your kids, please note that these symptoms may not be clear in their life at a young age, but then develop over the years or when they reach the age similar to the age at which the victim was once traumatised. It is your duty as a parent to identify these symptoms in your child.

Below are some symptoms similar to most children. Identify, if any, is common in the life of your child.

- Irritable
- Feeling helpless
- Unnecessarily quiet
- Eating disturbance
- Somatic complaints
- Loneliness
- Excessive mood swings, most of which might not be traceable to a physical event
- Fear
- Avoiding and withdrawing from social interactions
- Hurting themselves
- Emotional outburst
- Persistence sadness

- Withdrawal from social activities
- Talking about death
- Change in academic performance
- Frequent headaches and stomach aches
- Difficulty concentrating because their mind is easily distracted by their imaginations
- Disorder in perceptions and reasoning
- Difficulty understanding of perceptions of people
- Avoiding or missing school
- Hatred for social activities
- Unnecessary withdrawal from social activities'

2. Be sure of these emotional changes in your child. After identifying the potential changes in your child, it is helpful that you confirm whether these behaviours are not tied to any discomfort. Do confirm that you can ask their teachers, siblings, or even play groups. You can even take her on a trip to a different location to see if the behaviour persists. If it does, then it is time to employ the service of a therapist.

3. Seek a therapist

4. Become the first therapist; before you go about looking for a solution for your child's emotions, become the solution. It is your responsibility as a parent to read and research the term "inherited trauma" and how it can be traced back to your family history. So would guide you in relating to your child to get the best results and guide your child in healing from these inherited emotions. More on these topics will be released in our subsequent book. Send a message to receive an update when the book is released.

Cognitive Behavioural Therapy

CBT is an evidence-based approach to understanding and treating psychological problems. It is a structured, active form of therapy in which the client's goals are set in the beginning and addressed throughout therapy. Cognitive-behavioural therapy is based on four core assumptions:

- Your Thoughts, feelings, emotions, and physical reactions are all related. If you can change any of them, changes happen almost immediately in the others.
- Changes happen in small steps, most times not all at once. And the results may not manifest at first, but a steady step would bring lasting affects to the participant.
- Changing one's behaviour is a skill that requires practice and is more than just deciding to do something or make a change.
- Labelling our actions as "good" or "bad" won't help us get anywhere. Instead, it's more appropriate to think of our behaviour as "helpful or not helpful" or "healthy or unhealthy" to our overall aims.

Cognitive-behavioural therapy can be an effective tool for those struggling with inherited trauma, as it helps address their core issues and struggles. In addition, it promotes changes in patterns of thoughts, feelings, and emotions that affect the life of its victim, giving hope and joy to its victims.

CBT shows the link between thoughts, feelings, and actions of an individual and optimises them for better recovery.

Cognitive Processing Therapy (CPT).

Cognitive processing therapy is an aspect of cognitive-behavioural therapy (CBT). It was developed by Resick and Schnicke in the year 1992. It was created specifically to treat the PTSD of sexual abuse and molestation victims. However, it has been applied to various other traumas, including inherited family trauma. CPT entails writing about the traumatic event and reading it aloud to your therapist several times. This method of therapy is useful when dealing with guilt, self-blame, and negative emotions. Some exercises in CPT are listed at the end of the section. Some exercises include:

1. Write about the emotions and scenarios where they manifest repeatedly on a piece of paper. Repeating the same story repeatedly. Expressing it repeatedly can bring you to the point of realisation and healing.

2. *Rewrite the story to include the conditions in which you can gradually improve*. When writing, don't just write out the story to favour your suffering or present condition, but present it in ways that are comforting to your soul. Presenting it in healthy patterns with advice and comforting words It also involves writing it from a different perspective.

Dialectical Behaviour Therapy (DBT)

Dialectical behaviour therapy (DBT), developed by Marsha Linehan (1993), is a treatment that has great promise for trauma treatment. It has been used effectively to help people who have difficulty managing emotions and forming close relationships and with people who have thoughts of hurting themselves.

This mode of therapy comprises several aspects: mindfulness skills, interpersonal effectiveness, emotion regulation, and distress tolerance.

- MINDFULNESS SKILLS

Mindfulness is an effective skill in DBT that helps you build an awareness of the present moment, focusing your attention on your emotions, thoughts, and bodily sensations. It requires paying attention to what is going on, observing and describing your experiences, but doing so without judgment. Bringing the concept of mindfulness into psychology was quite a revolutionary move. Cognitive-behavioural therapy focuses on changing thoughts and emotions, whereas mindfulness simply focuses on developing awareness. Interestingly, developing mindfulness skills can help you deal with flashbacks and negative emotions. In addition, by paying attention to what is going on in the present moment, you can learn to ground yourself and better deal with most inherited traumas and PTSD symptoms. Check Worksheets 10, 12, 13, 18, and 25, which are focused on developing mindfulness in overcoming inherited emotions and traumas.

- INTERPERSONAL EFFECTIVENESS

Most people suffering from inherited emotions usually find it challenging to keep relationships or interact with others. Most of their challenges may feel like constantly fighting and arguing with other people. Such people usually have difficulty connecting with people they love and continually feel disappointed by others.

Every time they interact with others, they juggle between various priorities. Sometimes, building a healthy relationship with the other person is the most essential thing. Other times, the interaction is targeted at achieving a particular outcome, and other times, their self-respect is valued the most. Dialectical behaviour therapy skills can help you figure out your priorities.

Note that priorities during conversation and social interactions can change from time to time, so it's helpful that you pick out the goal of every interaction. Once you decide on your goal, you can use various techniques to get there.

For example, if reaching your aim is the most important thing (let's say you want a raise), use assertive communication skills and present a fair and balanced argument.

If your primary goal is to preserve a relationship (for example, if you are having an upsetting fight with your sister), you will communicate using a lot of empathy and understanding.

Also, if you are when your self-respect is compromised (for example, if someone asks you to lie), you remember your values and attempt to stick to them without apologies. By refusing or reacting in ways that communicate your value is being questioned.

- Emotion Regulation

Emotions can feel overwhelming. You may find yourself in situations where you have an uncontrollable amount of anxiety, anger, or sadness. Sometimes you may feel vulnerable to emotions, for example, when you are hungry, tired, or sick. Also, drinking too much alcohol or drugs can make you numb and emotionally unstable. One way to manage your emotions is to regularly address these issues. Good sleep, exercise, healthy nutrition, and cutting back on mood-altering substances can create the essential foundation for managing emotions and ensuring stability. Once that foundation is sound, you can then apply unique skills to handle these emotions when they come knocking.

You can do this by learning to judge whether your emotions are justified or are out of proportion to the situation. This will help you decide whether you want to try some active coping and problem-solving skills or practice some acceptance of the emotions.

- DISTRESS TOLERANCE

Distress tolerance skills help you manage moments of very intense emotions. They allow you to manage your feelings at the same moment they are being triggered, thus preventing them from being overwhelming or overreactive. For example, you might decide to distract yourself from emotional pain by doing things you enjoy or taking time out of the problematic situation and environment.

You can also diffuse your emotions by comparing yourself to others who have less than those who have more. Of course, sometimes no amount of distraction will be practical, helpful, or even possible. It is useful to think about ways to soothe yourself during these times. Different techniques work for other people. These include using imagery, prayer, relaxation, and breathing. You can also use positive self-talk to get you through difficult times. Finally, when distraction and soothing don't work, there is acceptance. Acceptance can be very difficult to accept. That's where acceptance and commitment therapy come into place.

Acceptance and Commitment Therapy

Acceptance and commitment therapy (ACT) is treatment that helps people observe their thoughts and emotions without judgment. Unlike DBT, acceptance and commitment therapy emphasize the need to identify your values and take action, regardless of your internal state (your thoughts or feelings). Acceptance and commitment therapy do not focus on changing thoughts or feelings, but emphasise how changing your behaviour can help you live a happier life. These skills also comprise two core areas: acceptance and mindfulness.

- ACCEPTANCE

Acceptance is an effective practice that guides you in accepting your emotions and their effects without minimizing, avoiding, or packaging them to seem normal. And thus, it appears to be the most difficult for many people. For example, a patient suffering from depression during acceptance therapy must accept that they are suffering from it and the effect of the depression on their mental health and stability. Such a person will weigh the consequences and observe the devastation that depression has caused in their social, physical, and emotional lives before deciding to stop using those pointers as a guide to ensuring effectiveness.

- MINDFULNESS

The mindfulness skills in the ACT are very similar to those found in DBT. Learning to notice the present moment and pay attention to your internal state is a critical component of mindfulness. Your thoughts and feelings are critical components of your inner state. When you learn to pay attention without pushing them away (acceptance), you will decrease your avoidance behaviors, thus enabling you to deal with the emotions accordingly.

- HOW WE SEE OURSELVES USING VARIOUS DESCRIPTIONS

Another important aspect of ACT is learning to explore how we see ourselves using various descriptions. For example, we may think of ourselves as "strong" or "independent." However, we might also see ourselves as depressed, traumatized, or damaged people. Our self-descriptions also involve our roles and what we do for a living. Acceptance and commitment therapy emphasize learning to gain some distance from these negative self-descriptions by separating your disadvantages from the advantage of becoming a better individual.

In the exercises below are some therapeutic worksheets that comprise different techniques and training effective in overcoming inherited family traumas and emotions.

Some therapeutic worksheets and exercises effective for your recovery

In this section, we would walk through various exercises based on cognitive behavioral therapy and dialectical behavioral therapy. If you're not sure which exercise to take, please go back to the beginning of this chapter.

Please note; the arrangement of these exercises is not in the algorithm and must not be followed according to the numbers. You should identify the one that suits your emotional healing and work with it until birth results.

Exercise 1: remaining calm.

This exercise guides you in managing and handling overwhelming emotions. In this section, we will employ deep breathing skills to achieve our goal of

controlling and managing these overwhelming emotions. Make copies of this worksheet or drop a sticker at this point to make it easier for returning to this point every day. You can as well note the page number.

Instructions

1. Choose a quiet place free from distractions. A place that was comfortable for meditation and quietness. The essence of these is to focus the senses to the point of internal unity and harmony, where you'll be able to master and take control of overwhelming emotions.

6. While sitting or standing, Place your hand on your belly and the other hand over your chest. Take a few regular breaths.

3. Now, as you take a breath, visualize the oxygen rushing in through your nose down to your lungs and abdomen. Taking deep breaths, imagine the air bringing freshness and newness as it moves to the lungs. resulting in your happiness and health

4. Next, focus on slowing down your breathing and taking count of your breaths both in and out. While doing these, you can decide to keep your eyes open or closed. Whichever is comfortable for you is to be in the presence at all points. Slowly and calmly breath in, then out... repeat the process repeatedly. To monitor your breath, you can say the word "one" to yourself as you inhale and say the words "life breath" to yourself as you exhale. Do this for twenty counts ("one life-breath" on the first breath, "two life-breath" on the second breath, do these for the third and the fourth until you reach the total counts. You can say these in your mind to avoid losing focus or getting distracted, or even running out of oxygen as you inhale and exhale.

5. Please note that you don't have to be a "perfect" breather! And it is entirely okay if your mind moves away or you get distracted during the process. When such an event occurs, quietly bring yourself back and

continue the process afresh. The aim is to bring your mind and focus to the point of wholeness and unity where worry and other emotional defects do not disturb you.

6. Repeat this exercise every morning for four weeks.

Note: the aim of doing these is to bring your body to the point of total control. If you can control your body through breathing and meditation, you can as well control your emotions when they become overwhelming. When faced with such an overwhelming situation, you can take a seat far away from the triggers and count your breath slowly. You must not strike the yoga pose or close your eyes. Take a seat, calm your nerves, and breathe… in and out, one life-breath per oxygen.

Exercise 2: Getting Active, building concentration on goals per time.

This section is a mindfulness exercise that enables you to focus on the present goal and be in the moment at all times. This exercise is effective, as it helps you take control of your thoughts and emotions. It prevents you from attributing inherited traumas to everyday activities or innocent individuals.

Here is an example from a young female graduate from a university in Ontario. The example would serve as a guideline to enable you to continue the exercise.

Before a task, just any task, Joy had to record the activity as instructed. She did it for her top three daily goals and took three others from her random daily activities. The core focus is on the emotions, before and after. Doing this helped her identify the core triggers of the inherited emotions, the bridging questions like why did I react this way, how did I handle this case, what was my core language, how did I feel, etc., and the triggers. This information can also trace the roots of the generation trauma and the incident that happened.

Here is an example:

> *My goal* is to write 3000 words in my manuscript, and I will do every morning for three days.
>
> *Body sensations before carrying out the activity:* I feel lazy and unable
>
> *Body sensations after exercise:* I feel better, happy, and energetic, especially knowing I have accomplished a goal.

Now it is your turn. In the exercises below, fill in the goals for the day and ask yourself these questions before and after

Repeat same for day two and day three. Print out over one copy for different tasks. Or use the compile a list in the appendix section of this book.

For today, write out atheist's three core goals, also show a time limit to prevent procrastination. Use the example above as a guide.

My goal is to (insert activity here) and I will continue these four (insert time frame here)

Your top three goals

1. _____

2. _____

3. _____

Goals from a random activity

1. _____

2.
_____

3.
_____

4.
_____

Before carrying out the activity, write them in the same order as the goals writing in the earlier section. I feel ....

1.
_____

2.
_____

3.
_____

body sensation after carrying out the activity

1.
_____

2.
_____

3.
_____

Get a journal or note and repeat these things every single day. You can also print out this page or put a sticker on this current page.

Exercise3: Observing and Changing

If you struggle with thoughts like "they will abandon me, they will sack me, everybody hates me, and so…" Then this section is for you. This section would guide you through identifying these traumatic thoughts and replacing them with more balanced, helpful alternatives. Use the worksheet to monitor your thoughts, anxieties, and unexplainable emotions for one week and come up with alternative ways to manage and handle these situations. At the end, rate these emotions, based on their intensity.

Example

> **Thought**: I am a terrible person. Everyone hates and avoids me.

> **The emotions I felt** while this thought was active were: Gloom and fear

> **How intense are these thoughts**? extremely ferocious and recurring

> **Alternative thoughts;** I might have experienced difficulties with friends or might have hurt a friend in time, but I still have friends that love and cherish our friendship. Maybe I'm not entirely the wrong person. People still want to be my friend. My best friend hasn't been made yet.

> **Emotions afterward**: I feel relief. Intensity afterward was reduced a little.

Now it is your turn.

Get your pen or pencil and fill in the spaces, constructing your alternative thoughts in the best possible way. Print out a copy of the page before writing.

1. Thought

_____

_____

_____

2. The Emotions I felt while this thought was active

_____

_____

3. How intense are these thoughts? Underline **anyone.**

   Quite severe   moderate   very severe   and reoccurring

4. Alternative thought

_____

_____

_____

_____

5. Emotions afterward

_____

_____

6. Emotions afterward

   Significantly reduced   Reduced a little   It didn't reduce.

If your emotions didn't reduce afterward, then

- Check your alternative thoughts

- To create another more soothing to your feelings
- By creating these, you identify with the strength and positivity in your life
- Look for the good, idealize if possible, but the more realistic, the better

Exercise 4: Observing and releasing these emotions

This section will teach you how to observe negative thoughts and emotions without judgment or self-criticism. This section applies to everyone struggling with intrusive thoughts, especially frightening or violent thoughts. It is also relevant to everyone working with overwhelming emotions. If you're one, follow the instructions below.

1. Locate a quiet place free from noise and distractions.

2. Sit in a comfortable chair. Your eyes can be open or closed, whichever is most comfortable. Set a timer for 4 minutes.

3. Recount the thoughts that come and go in your mind. If possible, bring the thought to light. At these points, you don't need to decide about whether to be judgmental. The thoughts might be ideal or real; allow them to flow and bring them to light.

4. After identifying this thought, carefully create or choose a metaphor describing a passing between your overwhelming thoughts and emotions and you, such as Here's an example of a metaphor:

RUSHING WATER

1. Imagine you are in a bountiful garden with green grass and tall trees. Also, in that garden is a stream with rushing water. You can hear the sounds of the water as it splatters with rocks and pebbles as it flows downstream.

2. Now imagine you walking towards this stream with these emotions and thoughts and emptying them all into the stream.

3. Imagine them flowing away from your fixed point as you wave a last goodbye, never to have them again. You can say goodbye, mentioning the emotions you feel. "Goodbye *anger,*" flow away. *I don't have you.*

4. *Goodbye depression, flow away. I don't have you.*

5. List them out and say goodbye to them. Say goodbye to your overwhelming emotions.

6. But keep in mind that as you say goodbye, you'd be wise to imagine the emotions fading into the midst, down the river, never to be found again.

7. Last, imagine yourself happy, the burden lifted, the overwhelming emotions gone. Imagine yourself freed from them all.

8. Now celebrate your freedom. You can repeat the following words: "Congratulations to me." I don't have the emotions again; they've all gone. I don't have anger. I am not depressed. I feel so happy and strong. Allow yourself to rejoice in the good and benefit of your freedom.

Dropping them all in the trash

1. Imagine you went hiking on a high hill together with these thoughts and emotions, but these emotions and thoughts are overwhelming and have become a burden to you.

2. Imagine going to a cliff, from which you can see a magnificent view of the world. Just below is a trash bin, big enough to contain all your emotions and thoughts.

3. Now imagine you dropping all these at the bottom of the Clift.

4. Imagine the emotions in a sack falling. Watch it as it keeps going down till it gets to the trash where it belongs.

5. Now, imagine the freedom that comes afterward; the feeling of easiness, the sense of relief, the relaxation in your muscles; imagine your body saying thank you as it smiles back at you.

Dropping them down from a plane

1. Let us say you are in an airplane, let us say a helicopter. Together with your emotions, you are sitting quietly at one point, but then the aircraft is losing balance, and the pilot is screaming. There is a trace of toxicity; he is shouting, and there are unwanted emotions weighing down the plane. You must discharge, or we will crash.

- Imagine the pilot repeating the words "discharge," or "we crash, discharge," or "we crash, discharge, discharge."

3. Imagine you walking towards the door yet holding the rails and handles so you won't fall, and quietly emptying your emotions and thoughts. Imagine emptying them into the wind, down to the oceans. Looking downwards, you see them fall and scatter as the winds toss them far below your standing and altitude.

4. Now imagine the pilot and everyone cheering and celebrating your success. The plane is calm and stable. You are free, relieved, happy, and relaxed. Imagine yourself comfortably sitting on the executive seats given to you as you heaved a sigh of relief.

You are done with the imaginative metaphors. It's time to log your results in the comments below. Please be honest and input the answers in the comments below.

1. How did you feel before the exercise?

_____

_____

_____

2. How did you feel after the exercise?

_____

_____

_____

3. How effective was this tool for your recovery?

Not effective   quite effective   Very effective

Exercise5: Observing Thoughts and Emotions

In this exercise, you will learn how to observe and identify your inherited traumatic language, experiences, and emotions, and distance your thoughts and emotions from them.

Instructions:

1. Choose a quiet place without distractions.

2. You can do these standing or sitting. Still, sitting has been proven to be the most effective. Locate a comfortable position, either a comfortable chair, or a comfortable environment that allows you to walk around. Whichever is best for you,

- Where you are now. You were focusing on the sensations in your body and the thoughts going through your mind. How do you feel at present? If you notice, you will feel calm, anxious, irritated, and so on.

While you keep noticing your present state, you also see that there is a part of you that is the observer: this is the part of you that can describe the sensations of your body and the thoughts going through your mind. This part of you is like the observer and is ever ready to observe your body sensations only if you bring it to focus on you.

4. Next, think about a time when you felt pleased. Think about what was going on. Who was there? What were your feelings? What was going on in your body? If possible, write them down.

While observing and trying to answer these questions, notice that part of you that is like a camcorder, constantly recording and following your inner state of mind and the memories attached.

5. Now, think about a time when you felt irritated or upset, or a time when these inherited emotions were affecting you. If possible, bring a memory to the limelight. Think about what was going on at that present time. Who was there? How did you feel at that point? What was going on in your body? While you answer, note the observant part of you, the one that is always recording your emotions, memories, and experiences.

6. I come back to the present. Take a moment to notice that "observer" part of yourself. Breathe calmly and allow the observant part of you to see your thoughts and feelings. You do not need to push away any thoughts or feelings. Simply allow yourself to observe what is going on.

You can repeat this exercise any time of the day or when the overwhelming emotions come around. Allow the observer to observe, then take note.

Log your practice below.

Observation Day 1

Notes on my thoughts, body sensations, and feelings before and after practice:

Describe The experience that happened. Who was there? What happened?

_____

_____

_____

_____

_____

_____

_____

_____

_____

_____

_____

_____

How did you feel when the incident occurred? Describe your body sensations?

_____

_____

_____

_____

_____

Exercise 6: overcoming the effects of inherited traumas

These exercises aim to understand how these inherited traumas and emotions have limited your life and further develop motivation to make changes.

Instructions:

1. Write in a few sentences <u>about how your inherited emotions, thoughts, feelings, or other symptoms have interfered with your ability to interact</u> with friends, family, colleagues, even spirituality. Be explicit and write everything you feel or think. How have your inherited emotions affected your life? How have they influenced your relationships or even your spirituality? Write them all down in the space provided.

2. Rate how important and how satisfying each of the several aspects of life (family, work, friends, and so on) is to you. Rate how important they are to you.

3. Use this information to develop an essential aspect of your life that has been affected by these emotions and that you want to improve.

4. Write four goals to pursue in the short term that will improve this aspect.

Example:

Most of the time, I struggle with depression and hatred for every family member. Like a curse, I always find peace and solitude outside my family. Not that they were harsh or did anything wrong, I just see myself hating them for no reason. I hate all of them and wish I was never part of the family. This traumatic emotion has affected my life to an extent. I despise it when friends talk about their

families or when I go to see them play with their children. I always conclude that it's a scam.

1. Family

How important are these to you?

Not Important   Somewhat Important, very _Important_

How satisfied are you with it?

Not Satisfied somewhat Satisfied   Very Satisfied

2. Work

How important are these to you?

Not Important   Somewhat Important   *Very Important*

How satisfied are you with it?

Not Satisfied   *Somewhat Satisfied*   Very Satisfied

3. Relationships

How important are these to you?

Not Important   Somewhat Important   *Very Important*

How satisfied are you with it?

Not Satisfied   Somewhat Satisfied   Very Satisfied

4. Spirituality

How important are these to you?

Not Important   *Somewhat Important*   Very Important

How satisfied are you with it?

Not Satisfied   Somewhat Satisfied   Very Satisfied

Area of Focus: Family

Goals:
   a. *to reconnect back to my family, letting go of these emotions,*
   b. *to love and cherish the bond we share as a family.*

Now it's your turn: answer the questions below HONESTLY

1. Ways my symptoms interfere with essential aspects of my life:

_____

_____

_____

_____

_____

_____

2. Rate the importance of each of the following aspects of your life and your satisfaction with them. With a pen or marker, circle the aspect that relates to you the most.

1. Family

How important are these to you?

   Not Important   Somewhat Important   Very Important

How satisfied are you with it?

   Not Satisfied   Somewhat Satisfied   Very Satisfied

2. Work

How important are these to you?

Not Important   Somewhat Important   Very Important

How satisfied are you with it?

Not Satisfied   Somewhat Satisfied   Very Satisfied

3. Relationships

How important are these to you?

Not Important   Somewhat Important   Very Important

How satisfied are you with it?

Not Satisfied   Somewhat Satisfied   Very Satisfied

4. Spirituality

How important are these to you?

Not Important   Somewhat Important   Very Important

How satisfied are you with it?

Not Satisfied   Somewhat Satisfied   Very Satisfied

3. from your ratings above, choose the most important area to you AND that you are least satisfied with. Choose the location that affects you the most and set goals for them. In the space below, input the areas of focus, may be family, work, friends, etc. write it boldly below.

Area of Focus: _____

4. Now, list at least three specific goals you want to achieve in the next two or three months. Goals that might enable you to overcome these traumas. What are these goals? Write them below.

_____

_____

_____

_____

_____

_____

_____

_____

Exercise 7: Identifying Emotions

The exercise aims to enable you to identify the traumatic emotions and inherited feelings, especially those emotions associated with unexplainable mood swings. In this section, we would create an emotional vocabulary list. Doing these would help you get back in touch with your emotions.

INSTRUCTIONS: Below is a list of possible different emotions experienced by various individuals suffering from inherited trauma. Highlight and read through the list. Add your own words to them.

Words related to love.	There are words related to joy.	There are words related to surprise.	There are words related to sadness.	Words that are related to danger.	Words that are related to fear.
Adoring	Happy	Amazed	Unhappy	Enraged Furious Fuming Livid Irate Upset Distraught Mad Bothered Annoyed	Anxious Nervous Tense Confused Worried Edgy Panicky Uneasy Apprehensive Horrified
Fond	Elated	Astonished	Hopeless		
Affectionate	Blissful Delighted	Astounded	Wistful		
Warm	Cheerful	Dazed	Pensive		
Compassionate	Hopeful Optimistic	Speechless	Despondent		
Sympathetic	Upbeat	Shocked	Disappointed		

Passionate	Confident	Flabbergasted	Miserable	_____	_____
	Satisfied			_____	_____
Infatuated	Comfortable		Overwhelmed	_____	_____
	Calm	_____			
Sentimental	Peaceful		Aggrieved		
	Content	_____			
Touched	Serene		Hurt		
	Pleased	_____			
Tender	Encouraged		Disturbed		
	Thrilled	_____			
_____	Excited		Inconsolable		
		_____			
_____			Guilty		
		_____			
_____			Ashamed		
		_____			
_____			Mortified		
		_____			
_____			Embarrassed		
			Reflective		
			Exhausted		
			Mournful		
			Regretful		

Exercise 8: Emotion Diary Cards

Emotional diary cards are check-up indicators used primarily to notice and label what you are feeling per time. Its use is unnecessary to change your emotions or create self-critic mediums. It is useful for noticing your feelings per time.

In this exercise, we would employ the tool of emotions diary cards to check up on our emotions at a various time intervals.

Instructions: pick and fill out any card at various time intervals three times a day. Using a few words to describe what you are feeling and how you are feeling now. Photocopy this page to create as many cards as you need.

My emotional diary cards

Date: _____

Time: _____

How do I feel;

_____

___

My emotional diary cards

Date: _____

Time: _____

How do I feel;

_____

My emotional diary card

Date: _____

Time: _____

How do I feel;

_____

___

My emotional diary card

Date: _____

Time: _____

How do I feel;

_____

___

My emotional diary card

Date: _____

Time: _____

How do I feel;

_____

___

My emotional diary card

Date: _____

Time: _____

How do I feel;

_____

___

Exercise 9: Managing Difficult Thoughts

This exercise is unique to those struggling with intrusive, aggressive, or violent thoughts. If your inherited emotions include distressing thoughts, this exercise is for you. Answer the questions that follow. In this session, we will learn how to identify and challenge complex thoughts.

Instructions:

1. For at least two weeks, write your distressing thoughts and emotions twice a day.

2. Also, identify the emotions that you are feeling at every point in the writing. In your report, summarise the first half of the day; what did you think from the time you woke up to 12pm, and in the next one, write out how you felt from 12pm till the time of writing, hopefully in the evening?

3. Try to come up with healthier ways to think about the situations that caused the overwhelming emotions, and you can do this by viewing the situation from a different perspective.

4. After viewing the situation from a different perspective, the next thing is to write your feelings again and see if they have changed.

5. But note that this exercise can be done in two forms. The first involves monitoring your emotions over time, while the other uses the exercise as a reference point for adjusting this thought and reducing the overwhelming emotions that accompany it. The notable difference between the two is that the first uses half of the day as a reference for checking. For others, time represents when the emotions and thoughts come.

Thought	Feelings before	Healthier Thought	Feelings

Date: 21/10/89	I feel hatred for everything	Everyone loves me, and I am only returning it with hate, which is inappropriate	I feel relief, and I feel better. I feel loved.
Time 1: 2;30pm			
Time 2: 7;00pm	The hate gradually reduced as I started taking the exercise. Somehow, I felt great.	Once I am done with the exercise, I'll get better and feel love for everything.	I feel Optimistic confident

Now it's your turn, fill in the required field in the spaces below,

Thought	Feelings before	Healthier Thought	Feelings after
Date: Time 1: Time 2:			
Date: Time 1: Time 2:			
Date: Time 1: Time 2:			

Date: Time 1: Time 2:		
Date: Time 1: Time 2:		
Date: Time 1: Time 2:		

Exercise 10: Connecting with Others

This exercise would guide you in becoming more aware of your daily interaction with others as you make conscious efforts to develop and nurturing effective relationships. The exercise would help you be more aware of the benefits of social interactions.

Instructions:

- In the spaces below, describe any specific interactions with people either in the past or in the future. Who was involved, what was said, and how did you react?
- What was your goal for the interaction?
- What strategy did you use, and reflections on how satisfied you were with how the encounter went?

Do this exercise once a day for at least seven days. Then, photocopy the next page, so you have more than enough space to express all your encounters and achieve the goal

Describe the Situation	What Was Your Goal?	What Strategies Did You Use?	Were You Satisfied with the Outcome? If Not, What Other Strategies Could You Have Used?
Example: I went to the school refectory and while eating, the director of nursing queried me for eating at an odd time, beyond the time allocated for feeding. My head was filled with these overwhelming emotions. I stood up, threw the food on the ground, and left.	I just wanted a place far from every human contact. And not really to eat.	I stood up, threw the food on the floor, and left.	I am not satisfied with the outcome. I regret my action.

I shouldn't have reacted the way I did

I should have calmly explained my present emotions to her without complicating the issue by throwing the food on the floor.

I should have kept calm and at least thought of what to say.

I should have explained to her I'm going through a bad day and needed just a place far from everything and everybody. |
| | | | |
| | | | |

Exercise 11: Changing Your self-criticising Thoughts

The goal of these exercises is to help you recognise your self-defeating and self-criticising thoughts and develop better, more loving ways of talking to yourself.

Instructions:

- Over many days, write as many of your invalidating thoughts as you can. Examine each of them to see if there is a more significant theme. Write them down in the spaces below.

- Then, when you have these thoughts, generate various methods of thinking based on the theme. These newly developed methods of thinking would help in opposing these thoughts.

- For easy reference, maintain a journal or a piece of paper with a note on which alternative concepts you'd like to recollect.

Example:

Here is an example with fortune a lab technician working with a prestigious university in North America, after observing his inherited emotions, which brought about some destructive intrusive thoughts. He came up with these in his worksheet.

The self-discriminating thoughts:
1. *If I don't do this, I'll be a complete failure and a disappointment to my family.*
2. *"I'm a terrible person.*
3. *Life is always hard.*

Notable themes:
Inferiority complex, tagged along with people's dependency

Alternative Thoughts:

I am a strong, confident, and well-organised man. Good planning and effective management are what I can do to execute any function. I do not need anybody's validation to make things work.

Things to Remember:
I can do it, and I am enough

Here is another example from Janeth, a young female in her prime struggling with having an anger issue. She quickly flares up at the slightest of all things and sees the world from a perspective beyond normal.

Invalidating Thoughts:
- *People are wicked*
- *Society is wicked, loose guard, and they will trample on you*

- *People would always take advantage of the weak,be weak, and they will trample on you*
- *Only the strong will survive*

Reoccurring themes:
fear of being humiliated or abused and even trampled upon by society.

Alternative Thoughts:
Society has both good, bad, and evil. And it all depends on me to accept the good always and let go of the rest. The world may not be evil. It all depends on my perspective.

Things to Remember
The world is not toxic or wicked, and I will always choose to accept the good and let go of the evil people. Also, to treat them well with love and acceptance without allowing my emotions to push them away.

Now it's your turn

What are those thoughts that reoccur? Write as many as you can remember in the space below? Also, write the notable themes and things to remember. Note that you can paste the things you remember in a place visible to you, write it on a paper sticker, and drop it by your bedside, on the door of the fridge, or even at the mirror. A place always visible to the human eyes. If the spaces provided are not enough, you can transfer these into a journal or notebook.

Invalidating Thoughts:

_____

_____

_____

_____

_____

_____

_____

_____

_____

Reoccurring themes:

_____

_____

_____

_____

_____

_____

Alternative Thoughts:

_____

_____

_____

_____

_____

_____

_____

Things to Remember

_____

_____

_____

_____

_____

Exercise 12: Planning

What if your overwhelming emotion or inherited trauma gets triggered? What would you do to tackle this? Would you react in the same obvious ways, or will you use the information in this book to tackle and challenge such reactions? In

this section, you will learn to identify and plan for emotionally upsetting situations and their triggers.

Instructions:

Think about potential challenges you may face in the coming week or day and how your emotions will react to them.

Consider how you could mix your emotional and rational responses to create a defence mechanism that would act as a coping mechanism.

You can duplicate this worksheet and use it at the start of each week to prepare for emotionally tricky or demanding situations.

Here is an example:

I'm concerned that my anger may flare up when my mom tries to talk to me about things, I feel like doing.

Emotional reaction: get angry, talk to her in ways she won't like, and leave her

Rational reaction: The earlier I realise it may be for my good, the better for me. My mum might do it in my best interest. Let me at least observe the condition from her perspective, and it might be worth it.

Combined reaction: consciously meet my mom and stay in control for as long as I can. If, by any means, the overwhelming emotions come up, I must and should quietly leave without making her feel upset, being harsh, or even allowing my anger to interfere. I can do this for as much time as I like till my body adjusts to it.

Evaluation of the plan (after the situation): It went well. On the first trial, she said nothing, but when I went the second and third time, the advice popped up. I tried as much as possible to remain calm. I did it to the point of exhaustion, and

when I felt I couldn't take it anymore, I quietly left, using a call as an excuse. After that, I repeated the steps till I reached the point of total control. At that point, I could see from her perspective.

Now it's your turn

Anticipated Challenge:

_____

_____

_____

_____

_____

_____

_____

_____

Emotional reaction:

_____

_____

_____

_____

_____

_____

Rational reaction:

_____

_____

_____

_____

_____

Combined reaction:

_____

_____

_____

_____

_____

Evaluation of plan (after the situation)

_____

_____

_____

_____

Exercise 13: improving your social support skills

In this section, you will identify and appreciate core areas where you have good social support, also noticing other core areas where expand your support network.

Instructions: Answer the questions below based on your experiences. Use the answers to determine your strength in those areas, checking if you want to increase your support in those areas or not.

1. Do you have friends you socialise with regularly (at least once a month)? How many friends do you associate with without these emotions interfering?

   None   Very few (1 or 2)   Some (3 to 5)   A lot (over 5)

2. How satisfied are you with this area of support? (Circle one

   Not at all satisfied   Somewhat satisfied   Very satisfied

3. Do you have family members who you socialise or interact with regularly (at least once a month)? Are their family members that boost your emotions by making you happy?

   None   very few (1 or 2)   Some (3 to 5)   A lot (over 5)

4. How satisfied are you with this area of support? (Circle one

   Not at all satisfied   Somewhat satisfied   Very satisfied

5. Do you attend activities at least once a month (for example, church, clubs, other hobbies in a social setting) where you interact with other people?

   None   Very few (1 or 2)   Some (3 to 5)   A lot (over 5)

6. How satisfied are you with this area of support? (Circle one

       Not at all satisfied   Somewhat satisfied   Very satisfied

7. Do you have people you can rely on when you need things (help, social support, financial support, etc.

     None   Very few (1 or 2)   Some (3 to 5)   A lot (over 5)

8. How satisfied are you with this area of support? (Circle one

       Not at all satisfied   Somewhat satisfied   Very satisfied

9. Do you have friends in your life who you can count on for emotional support? (For example, to listen to you when you have a problem, give you advice when you want it, and tell you they care about you.

     None   Very few (1 or 2)   Some (3 to 5)   A lot (over 5)

10. How satisfied are you with this area of support? (Circle one

       Not at all satisfied   Somewhat satisfied   Very satisfied

Need More Help?

This section would guide you in determining areas where you need help; below is a list of different inherited traumatic emotions. Check the answers that apply to you by underlining yes or no where applicable. If the number of yes is over five at the end, you may need a therapist.

Do I have frightening nightmares or intrusive, disturbing thoughts on harming myself or going extreme in hurting others	YES	NO
Do I feel the overwhelming emotions of committing suicide	YES	NO

Do I find it extremely difficult relating with others	YES	NO
Have you ever attempted suicide?	YES	NO
Do you keep seeing frightening or disturbing images?	YES	NO
Have my overwhelming emotions caused me to break the law or do extreme violent things	YES	NO
Have you ever engaged in risky or unprotected sex?	YES	NO

From your answers above, locate the ones that apply to you and apply the measures

From above, how many marks did you say yes to?	Solutions and likely outcomes
1 or 2	May not need a therapist. Please create a plan for recovery. Expand your knowledge by reading the recommended books and following the exercise where necessary.
2, 3 or 4	A little severe, and may worsen visit a therapist now
5 and 6	It might be disturbing. Visit a therapist now.

CHAPTER SIX

The Other Side Of Your Fears

Most time, after a good therapeutic session, reading a book, or attending a seminar or webinar addressing your core struggles, especially those related to your mental health and general wellness, You feel all good and energised, but a few days later, you're back to the question: is it working? Was it effective? Am I healing? Other times, you are stuck between an inner critic condemning and assuming you were wasting your time.

The core question always remains; how do we get to the other side of this fear, conquer our fears, heal ourselves for good, and enjoy the lasting effects that come with the benefits?

From previous chapters, we identified the severity of inherited family trauma on its victims and how to overcome them. For good. We introduced a series of exercises, practices, affirmations, and routines to enable you to overcome these inherited emotions for good. In this chapter, we will wrap up by listing some important ways of ensuring the content of this book manifests in your life. The chapter is to help you remain free from these inherited emotions.

Your mind, the powerhouse

You are what you think. Your mind, emotions, and actions all work in a similar pattern. They follow the same sequence of operations. What you believe determines how you feel, and what you think determines how you behave. Inherited emotions won't be forever lost without a renewal of the mind. And a renewal of the mind starts with a change of perspective. Your perspective must change for you to be completely free. You can read all the books and attend all

the therapy in the world. If your mind isn't renewed, then every step you take is useless. Your mind is the powerhouse. Adopt new practices to train your mind in order to emerge victorious.

Steps to ensure your mind aligns with your recovery

1. **Keep note:** your mind is an ample space where different thoughts are filtered, ignored, or forever accepted. Note-taking is a positive way of ensuring your mind keeps specific kinds of information. Words are written to last longer in the mind than thoughts. Your brain continuously transmits things written as being important.

   While working through the workbook, you will notice spaces for writing. If you followed the instructions and wrote in the columns required without missing a point or two, then you are ready. Your brain sees this action as a joyous task in delivering your desired result. And unconsciously align your thinking with patterns of behavior that are diametrically opposed to the wrongs you wrote about.

2. **Positive affirmations (**affirmations are words you say to yourself). They either improve you or demote you. They can build you up as well as destroy you. What you say continuously affects your mind and public life. If you believe you will be tremendous and constantly declare positive and great things, the world will bring your declaration and expectations to you sooner than later. Positive affirmations are constructive signals sent to the brain and whole-body system, enforcing a supernatural attraction between the declared and the present self. Be careful of your affirmations; they determine the level of results you will gain after therapeutic exercise. Throughout this book, affirmations were employed, from releasing the hurt back to the owner to enforce freedom from their guilt and pains. Affirmation is mandatory for adequate recovery. Work through the exercise one more time, highlight the essential and daily affirmations, and repeat them as often as possible. Doing this sends a signal attracting positive

things to the world and a significant release of negative emotions and behaviours.

MANAGING THE INNER CRITIC

Work through the exercise one more time, highlight the essential and daily affirmations, and repeat them as often as possible. Doing this sends a signal of attraction of positive things to the world and a significant release of negative emotions and behaviors.

1. **Restructuring your beliefs and thought patterns;** your thoughts influence your emotions, and your emotions influence your actions. Your beliefs are positive or negative thoughts and ideologies you have about yourself. Most of the time, these beliefs are limiting factors preventing the full recovery of victims suffering from inherited emotions and other effects of inherited trauma. Restructuring your beliefs and thinking patterns requires changing some ideologies you once had and embracing healthy and acceptable behaviors beneficial for your healing.

   Jane always believed staying alone was the best way to gain peace of mind. Unfortunately, this has prevented her from making new friends and even socializing. She had this fear that knowing and dating many people would only bring misunderstandings, quarrels, envy, etc which might affect her peace of mind. Little did she know that her fears and worries were tied to inherited emotions associated with a trauma her grandfather had once experienced. During therapy, she was walked through the steps to overcome these traumas, but her healing didn't emerge immediately until she attempted to restructure her mind and beliefs. She forced her mind to discard the idea that safety comes only when you're alone. And attempted to improve her communication skills. She did this by noting the positive benefit of having the right people around her.

2. **Enforcing new rules and behavior patterns**, all humans are controlled by laws and regulations, including the human brain and internal systems. Inherited traumas, including those encoded in the DNA, action patterns, and others, can be regulated and restructured to accept ways geared towards achieving your desired goals. Enforcing new rules requires doing things that will positively influence your habits and behaviors, thus affecting your actions, thinking patterns, and emotions. New rules can be placed on your daily routine, social life, emotional life, and all other parts of human life.

An individual suffering from overwhelming emotions can reduce the triggers, thus preventing her from going back to her former self. Those suffering from depression can change their daily activities and enforce the best alternative for socializing and breaking the belief that was once the norm. Now that you have, you must believe and align your thoughts, emotions, and life to be like an individual freed from these inherited emotions.

INTERNAL AND EXTERNAL TRIGGERS OF INHERITED TRAUMA

1. **Your environment,** to a large extent, determines the level of results you get from recovery. Most of the time, close to the end of a therapeutic session, people are advised to avoid the wrong environment or are equipped with coping skills for managing their emotions and staying in control. To enjoy lasting healing, avoid hostile environments or environments that would remind you of your former self, and if you're to stay, ensure you equip yourself with healthy coping skills.

2. **Your friends and family,** the bible says a company of fools will be destroyed. Your company and association determine the outcome you gain. An individual freed from social anxiety must avoid every hindrance to meeting new friends and exploring new environments. Individuals suffering from depression must also ensure that they are free of anyone, whether friends or family, who will push them back into their old shell.

3. **Inner critics and self-image** are internal triggers of inherited emotions that could disrupt the general wellbeing and healing of individuals with inherited trauma. What are the voices in your head saying, and how do you see yourself after healing? Do you still see yourself as inferior, unable, or unattractive? Is the voice in your head interfering with your enjoyment of your new form, or are they reminding you of your past? Irrespective of the case, let it go, flush it out. You are a transformed individual with healthy coping skills and boundaries. You are not limited by the vague image presented to you by your mind. The person you used to be is no longer the same.

Declare Your Independence

Declaring your independence involves proclaiming the best of everything you want. It is evoking the universe to grant you your earnest desires and expectations, ensuring you remain completely free. In one of the bestselling books by Joel Osteen, a prominent preacher in the United States, I *declare 31 promises to speak over your life. He defines a* declaration as those words we send out to the universe that determine the direction we want our life to go.

When you declare positively, the universe is compelled to bring forth whatever you have declared. Like a magnet, a declaration attracts the best of results for you. To remain free from the effects of inherited emotions and traumas, you must declare your freedom. You must say the opposite of whatever you once experienced. You must positively declare your expectations into existence. If you're going through depression, you must start declaring your freedom from depression by declaring the opposite of depression. Here is an example.

* I am free.
* I am transformed.
* I do not have depression.

* I am a happy and jovial person.
* Maintaining healthy relationships is the thing I have good friends for.

From the example above, it is noticeable that the declarations are always channeled to bring forth the best of experience for a person. What inherited emotions are you free from? Declare them positively. Here is a list of declarations. You can add them to your list of declarations.

1. I am free.
2. I am transformed.
3. I am unique.
4. I am changed.
5. I am different.
6. I am not afraid of anyone.
7. I am a new individual.
8. There is a new life for me.
9. There are healthy boundaries for me.
10. My inherited emotions have been returned to the world.
11. I am creative.
12. Everything I need is in my possession.
13. I am successful.
14. I am equipped.
15. Nothing bad can happen to me.
16. Everything good becomes my portion.
17. My transformation has started already.
18. I can't be sick or suffer as a victim.
19. I am loved.
20. The best is me.
21. Everything missing in my life has been transformed.
22. I have everything I ever wanted.
23. I can never be angry.
24. I can never be depressed.
25. Depression is gone for good.
26. I am renewed.
27. My choices are always right.
28. I am loved.
29. I am unique and beautiful.
30. There are not two like me in the world.
31. I am special.
32. I deserve to be celebrated and loved.

33. I don't have anxiety.

34. I am not a failure.

35. I have emerged.

36. There is a difference between my former self and now.

37. I am the best.

38. This year would be the best for me.

39. I am loved.

40. I am not different. I am better.

Now it's your turn to declare your independence. In the spaces below, whiteout positive declarations are effective for your healing and read them to yourself as often as possible.

1. _____

2. _____

3. _____

4. _____

5. _____

6. _____

7. _____

8. _____

9. _____

10. _____

11. _____

12. _____

Your declaration could be a motivation to other persons. Drop a screenshot of your list as a review for your favorite bookstore. Let other readers get insight and add to their catalog of declarations. Take a snapshot of the **previous page** containing your list of positive affirmations and post on your favorite bookstore.

Define and Set Healthy Limits and Boundaries

Boundaries are everything. They protect you from the toxicity of other people as well, preserving your peace and wellbeing, and your renewed state of mind after the transformation. It is of great essence that you create healthy boundaries as a defense mechanism against intrusive thoughts, emotions, and people who might assume you to be your former self or try to intimidate, bully, or persuade you into returning to your shell. You must create boundaries around your emotions, comfort, mental wellbeing, and even your belongings. Doing so would ensure the lasting effect of your healing from inherited family trauma and emotions.

Dr Corin Wellington

APPENDIX

Dear reader

Thank you for reading to this point. I am confident that the tools listed in this book at one point were effective for your recovery.

Healing from inherited trauma may not be a onetime pill forever healing solution, but requires a step-by-step gradual approach to ensuring your freedom is satisfied. It is necessary that you treat this manual as a handbook, an effective guide necessary for your healing. Go through the content, again and again, redo the exercise. Proclaim the affirmations and take on the daily routines. Don't be in a hurry to finish, but have a tracker to ensure you are on track and your healing is progressive.

Please note that because this workbook solved the problem of inherited family trauma, it is no place to assume the role of a therapist. In severe cases, especially if the book didn't provide the needed help, it is advisable to meet a qualified therapist who would give you additional help and coach you up in ensuring you fully recover from the effect of inherited family trauma.

From the next page are some additional guides that would be of great importance to your recovery.

Recommended text

> It didn't start with you; how inherited family trauma shapes who we are and how to end the cycle. A book by mark Wilson
> The body keeps the score; brain, mind, and body in the healing of trauma; a book by Bessel van der Kolk M.D
> Adult children of emotionally immature parents how to heal from a distance, rejecting or self-involved parents; a book written by Lindsay C. Gibson

Recommended websites

This is among the best therapeutic site for getting useful information for overcoming these traumas. Founded in 1967, they have kept a sound track record of high content useful information for treating all kinds of mental health challenges.

Ensemble Therapy is a useful site that contains tons of information for overcoming inherited trauma, though their core focus is on children, teens, and their families. They also have offices in Austin, Texas.

➤ www.health.com

Health.com is a useful site for getting useful therapeutic advice and information for overcoming social anxiety. It is among the most useful and most visited sites that rank 88th among Health Information sites.

➤ www.google.com
Google Is the biggest and most popular search engine where every information is found. The search engine can produce a useful result, but it's based on what you search. For overcoming social anxiety, it is helpful that you use the right keywords for searching and getting answers.

➤ www.quora.com

Quora is a **community-based questions and answers website and app**. Where Users post questions on any topic and other users respond with the most appropriate of all answers. Through Quora, you can get useful information for overcoming inherited trauma.

➤ Other sites include

www.Childtrauma.org

www.ptsd.va.com

www.traumacentre.org

www.acestudy.org

Recommended therapeutic offices and where to get help

Go to www.therapyroute.com and search by location, locate any therapy suitable for you and book an appointment

The second method, using your browser search for www.goodtherapy.org, input your city and search, it will provide a list of therapists around your location. Choose the one suitable for your healing and book an appointment.

You can as well visit www.psychologytoday.com and book an appointment with a therapist

Medicines and healthy living

Patients with severe symptoms of depression, anxiety, anger, sleep disturbances, and nightmares can benefit from medications such as antidepressants and antianxiety medications. Typically, medication is prescribed by a medical professional, such as a family physician or psychiatrist, and is used with other treatments, like counselling or psychotherapy.

Research has shown that Post Traumatic Stress Disorder management and wellness can be improved by living a healthy lifestyle. Healthy living comes because of getting regular exercise, adopting a balanced diet, managing stress, getting good sleep, taking part in the community, and receiving social support.

Your healing is sure.

Dr Corin Wellington

APPENDIX

REFERENCE

1. Examination of the Prezygotic Hypothesis from Maternal Age Influences on Twins," Behavioural

2. Genetics 28(2) (1998): 101

3. Thomas W. Sadler, Longman's Medical Embryology, 9th ed. (Baltimore: Lippincott Williams & Wilkins

4. Finch and Loehlin, "Environmental Influences That May Precede Fertilization," 101–2

5. Tracy Bale, "Epigenetic and Transgenerational Reprogramming of Brain Development," Nature ReviewsNeuroscience, 16 (2015): 332–44; doi:10.1038/nrn3818

6. Bruce H. Lipton, "Maternal Emotions and Human Development," Birth Psychology,https://birthpsychology.com/free-article/maternal-emotions-and-human-development

7. Bruce H. Lipton, PhD, The Wisdom of Your Cells: How Your Beliefs Control Your Biology (Louisville,CO: Sounds True, Inc., 2006), audiobook, Part 3

8. Alice Park, "Junk DNA—Not So Useless After All," Time, September 6, 2012

9. Danny Vendramini, "Noncoding DNA and the Teem Theory of Inheritance, Emotions and InnateBehavior," Medical Hypotheses 64 (2005): 512–19, esp. p. 513, doi:10.1016/j.mehy.2004.08.022

10. Park, "Junk DNA—Not So Useless After All.

11. Michael K. Skinner, "Environmental Stress and Epigenetic Transgenerational Inheritance," BMC

12. Vendramini, "Noncoding DNA and the Teem Theory of Inheritance, Emotions and Innate Behavior," Danny Vendramini, "Paper 5 of 5: The Teem Theory of NonMendelian Inheritance

13. Tori Rodriguez, "Descendants of Holocaust Survivors Have Altered Stress Hormones," ScientificAlisha Rouse, "Holocaust Survivors Pass the Genetic Damage of Their Trauma onto Their children.dailymail.co.uk/sciencetech/article3206702/Holocaust-survivors-pass-genetic-damage-trauma-children-researchers-find.html

14. Patrick McGowan, et al., "The Legacy of Child Abuse," Headway 4(1) (2009), McGill University

15. Jamie Hackett, "Scientists Discover How Epigenetic Information Could Be Inherited," Research, University of Cambridge, www.cam.ac.uk/research/news/scientists-discover-howepigenetic-information-could-be-inherited

16. Brian G. Dias and Kerry J. Ressler, "Parental Olfactory Experience Influences Behavior and Neural Structure in Subsequent Generations," Nature Neuroscience 17 (2014): 89–96, doi:10.1038/nn.3594

17. Hackett, "Scientists Discover How Epigenetic Information Could Be Inherited. Katharina Gapp, et al., "Implication of Sperm RNAs in Transgenerational Inheritance of the Effects of Early Trauma in Mice," Nature Neuroscience 17 (2014): 667–69, doi:10.1038/nn.3695

18. Nervous System: New Molecular Targets," CNS Neurological Disorder Drug Targets 5(4) (August2006): 453–79. Hiba Zaiden, Micah Leshem, and Inna Gaisler-Salomon, "Prereproductive Stress to Female Rats AltersCorticotropin Releasing Factor Type 1 Expression in Ova and Behavior and Brain CorticotropinReleasing Factor Type 1 Expression in Offspring," Biological Psychiatry 74(9) (2013): 680–87,doi:10.1016/j.biopsych.2013.04.014.

19. Max-Planck-Gesellschaft, "Childhood Trauma Leaves Mark on DNA of Some Victims: Gene2012. Patrick O. McGowan, et al., "Epigenetic Regulation of the Glutocorticoid Receptor in Human BrainAssociates with Childhood Abuse," Nature Neuroscience 12(3) (March 2009): 342–48, pp. 342–45

20. Hackett, "Scientists Discover How Epigenetic Information Could Be Inherited."Rachel Yehuda, et al., "Transgenerational Effects of Posttraumatic Stress Disorder in Babies of MothersEric Nestler, MD, PhD, "Epigenetic Mechanisms of Depression," JAMA Psychiatry 71(4) (2014)

21. David Sack, MD, "When Emotional Trauma Is a Family Affair," Where Science Meets the Steps (blog), Psychology Today, www.psychologytoday.com/blog/where-science-meets-thesteps/201405/when-emotional-trauma-is-family-affair

22. Virginia Hughes, "Sperm RNA Carries Marks of Trauma," Nature 508 (April 17, 2014): 296–97,www.nature.com/news/sperm-rna-carries-marks-of-trauma-1.15049

23. Linda G. Russek and Gary E. Schwartz, "Feelings of Parental Caring Predict Health Status in Midlife: A35-Year Follow-up of the Harvard Mastery of Stress Study," Journal of Behavioral MedicineP. Graves, C. Thomas, and L. Mead, "Familial and Psychological Predictors of Cancer," CancerDetection and Prevention

24. David Chamberlain, Windows to the Womb: Revealing the Conscious Baby from Conception to Birth(Berkeley, CA: North Atlantic Books, 2013), 180

25. Michael Bergeisen, interview with Rick Hanson, "The Neuroscience of Happiness," Greater Good: TheScience of a Meaningful Life, September 22, 2010,http://greatergood.berkeley.edu/article/item/the_neuroscience_of_happiness

26. Bert Hellinger, No Waves Without the Ocean: Experiences and Thoughts (Heidelberg, Germany: CarlAuer International, 2006)

27. Rick Hanson, "How to Trick Your Brain for Happiness," Greater Good: The Science of a Meaningful

28. Thomas Verny, with John Kelly, The Secret Life of the Unborn Child (New York: Simon & Schuster,1981),

29. Ken Magid and Carole McKelvey, High Risk: Children Without a Conscience (New York: BantamBooks, 1988)

30. Edward Tronick and Marjorie Beeghly, "Infants' Meaning-Making and the Development of Mental Health Problems," American Psychologist

INDEX

Enjoyed the book? Check out more from the publisher

INHERITED EMOTIONS;
HOW FAMILY TRAUMA
AFFECTS YOUR LIFE

ENDING THE CYCLE OF
INHERITED EMOTIONS; 10
PROVEN WAYS OF OVERCOMING
INHERITED FAMILY TRAUMA

REMAIN FREE FROM INHERITED
EMOTIONS; INTRODUCING DBT,
CBT AND ACT N OVERCOIING
INHERITED TRAUMA

BE THE FIRST TO GET THIS BOOK ONCE PUBLISHED AND stay
updated on the latest series on this book by sending us a mail at
overcomefamilytrauma@gmail.com.

On receival we would send you a bundle of free books effective for
your overcoming inherited family trauma.

Made in the USA
Las Vegas, NV
18 September 2022

55527567R00109